THE BEST OF
WHAT'S COOKING

BURT WOLF

THE BEST OF
WHAT'S COOKING

BURT WOLF

ACORN ASSOCIATES LTD.
30 LINCOLN PLAZA
NEW YORK, N.Y. 10023

CONTENTS

POULTRY

MEAT

PASTA & RICE

VEGETABLES

SALADS

SAUCE & DRESSINGS

DESSERTS

CAKES, PIES, TARTS & COOKIES

INTRODUCTION

For the past fifteen years, I have been lecturing, writing and making television shows about good food and drink. I have traveled around the world with my crew recording recipes, tips and techniques from many skilled professionals. We have produced over 2,000 segments which are now being broadcast in all fifty states, Puerto Rico, Australia, Canada, South America and Japan. The 100 recipes in this book were selected from my reports. The original recipes have been tested and modified for use in a home kitchen.

My objective was to produce a book that was informal and modest, containing a series of recipes that are worth their time, effort and money.

None of this could have been achieved without the great cooks, chefs, hotel owners and restaurants who have shared their extensive knowledge with me.

Special thanks for the production of the book must go to Barbara Albright, Emily Aronson, Mary Campagna, Mary Elges, Anna Friedlander, Ron Klayman, May Mendez, Mardee Haidin Regan, Joel Schwartz, Eugene Stuttman and Ira Tumpowsky.

A note on the number of servings for each recipe:

The recommendation that a specific recipe will make a given number of servings is only a "rough" estimate.
A particular recipe will have a very different serving yield for my teenage son and his friends than it will for a group of fashion models on a weight-loss diet.

I have always believed that the number of servings a recipe will yield depends on how good the final dish tastes. I once had an ice cream recipe that turned out so well it only served one...me! On the other hand, if people don't like the taste of something...a small quantity could serve thousands.

APPETIZERS

JAMES BEARD'S ONION COCKTAIL SANDWICHES

1 loaf white bread, sliced
1 cup mayonnaise
2 large sweet mild onions, thinly
     sliced
1 cup fresh parsley, minced

1. Using a 2-inch biscuit cutter or a drinking glass with a 2-inch rim, cut out out a circle from the center of each slice of bread.

2. Spread each round with a thin coating of mayonnaise.

3. Arrange a slice of the onion on half of the bread rounds and top with the remaining rounds, mayonnaise side down.

4. Lightly brush the edge of each little sandwich with mayonnaise, then roll the edge in minced parsley.

Makes about 10 sandwiches

BUYING ONIONS
Whatever kind of onion you buy, pick ones that are firm and dry. The outside should have a crunchy, crackly texture; it should feel papery. There should be no soft spots, no wetness and the flatter the stem end the better. Moisture is the enemy of stored onions. Keep them in a dry place away from potatoes which give off moisture. It's also good to store them in a dark place.

LITTLE HOT CORNED BEEF
AND SAUERKRAUT MEATBALLS

¼ pound unsalted butter
1 medium onion, finely chopped
1½ pounds cooked corned beef,
   shredded, or two 12-ounce cans
   corned beef
1 tablespoon fresh parsley,
   minced
1 teaspoon dry mustard
1 teaspoon salt
1 cup all-purpose flour
1 cup milk
1 pound sauerkraut, drained well
   and finely chopped
2 eggs
¼ cup water
2 cups fine dry bread crumbs
Vegetable oil for deep-frying

1. Melt the butter in a large saute pan. Add the onions and cook until translucent, about 3 to 5 minutes. Add the corned beef and the parsley and cook for 5 minutes. Stir in the mustard, salt and flour. Gradually add the milk and cook, stirring constantly, until thickened, about 5 minutes.

2. Add the sauerkraut to the meat mixture. Mix thoroughly, cover and refrigerate for 2 hours.

3. Shape the mixture into ½-inch balls.

4. Beat the eggs with the water. Place the bread crumbs in a shallow dish. One at a time dip the balls into the egg mixture and then roll in the bread crumbs.

5. Heat 2 inches of the oil in a wide, heavy saucepan to a temperature of 375°F. Fry the meatballs until golden brown.

Makes about 4 dozen

BUFFALO CHICKEN WINGS

30 chicken wings
Vegetable oil for deep-frying
¼ pound unsalted butter
½ cup hot pepper sauce
Blue cheese dressing, for dipping
  (See page 76)
Celery sticks

1. Separate the chicken wings at the joint and discard the tips.

2. Heat 2 inches of the oil in a wide saucepan or a high-sided saute pan to 375°F. Deep-fry the chicken wings for 8 minutes, or until golden brown.

3. While the chicken cooks, in a medium skillet, melt the butter and stir in the hot sauce. Set aside.

4. When the chicken is cooked, drain on paper towels and add to the hot butter mixture. Toss and serve with blue cheese dressing or another dressing as a dipping sauce and celery sticks.

Makes about 6 servings

DEEP-FRYING TIPS
When you are deep-frying foods, they must be fully submerged in deep oil or fat. This will allow the entire surface of the food to be quickly sealed by the fat. The natural moisture and juices are held in.

The oil should be at a temperature of 375°F. for most foods. The best way to be sure the temperature is correct is to attach a deep-frying thermometer to your pan.

GUACAMOLE

2 ripe avocados
2 tomatoes, cored, seeded and
  chopped
1 small white onion, chopped
2 chile serranos, trimmed,
  seeded and finely chopped
2 sprigs coriander, stemmed and
  chopped (optional)
½ teaspoon salt
Tortilla chips

1. Cut the avocados in half and discard the pits. With a spoon, scoop the flesh into a bowl and mash with a fork.

2. Stir in the tomatoes, onion, chile serranos, coriander, if used, and salt.

3. Serve at room temperature with tortilla chips.

Makes about 2 cups

AVOCADOS AND NUTRITION
Avocados are highly digestible and provide vitamins A, several B vitamins, C and E. There is a good amount of iron in avocados and they are low in sodium. Avocados, however, are rich in fruit oil which is a saturated fat. If you are on a low-saturated fat diet (a good idea for most people), limit your intake of avocados.

YOGURT CHEESE SPREAD
WITH SCALLIONS AND WALNUTS

8 cups plain yogurt
½ cup scallions, finely minced
1½ cups coarsely chopped
    walnuts
Salt and freshly ground black
    pepper

1. Line a colander with several large layers of dampened cheesecloth, letting enough of the cheesecloth hang over the edges to fold back over the surface of the yogurt.

2. Place the yogurt in the colander, cover with the excess cloth, set the colander in a bowl and refrigerate overnight. The moisture in the yogurt will drain out and the volume of the yogurt will reduce by half.

3. If you discover that the yogurt has become overly thick, beat in a little of the liquid that drained into the bowl. Stir in the scallions, walnuts, and salt and pepper to taste.

4. Mound the mixture in a dish or bowl. Serve with toasted pita bread or crackers, or use the mixture to stuff celery or endive spears.

Makes about 4 cups

CHEESE STRAWS

8 ounces sharp cheddar cheese,
   finely shredded
¼ pound unsalted butter
1¾ cups sifted all-purpose flour
¼ teaspoon salt
¼ teaspoon Cayenne pepper
½ teaspoon Tabasco sauce

1. In a bowl, beat together the cheese and butter until well blended.

2. Sift the flour, salt, and Cayenne directly onto the cheese-butter mixture. Add the Tabasco sauce and mix until thoroughly blended. Form the dough into two large discs, cover with plastic or foil and refrigerate for 1 hour.

3. Preheat the oven to 425°F.

4. Using a rolling pin on a lightly floured surface, roll out each portion of dough about ⅛-inch thick. Cut the dough into 3 x ½-inch rectangular strips and carefully place the strips on an ungreased baking sheet.

5. Bake the cheese straws for 8 minutes. Remove to a rack and let cool. If not serving the cheese straws immediately, store in an airtight container.

Makes 2 dozen

NOTE: This dough can be kept on hand in the freezer for up to 3 months and rolled out as needed.

FRIED FONTINA CHEESE

1½ pounds Fontina cheese
Freshly ground black pepper
1 cup all-purpose flour
4 eggs, well beaten
1½ cups fine dry bread crumbs
Vegetable oil, about 1 quart for
   deep-frying

1. Cut the cheese into finger-size strips.

2. Sprinkle the cheese strips with pepper. Dip each strip into the flour to thoroughly coat it, then into the beaten eggs and then into the bread crumbs. Coat the cheese strips again using only the beaten eggs and bread crumbs.

3. Pour 1-inch of the vegetable oil into a heavy, deep saucepan. Place a deep-frying thermometer into the oil and heat to 365°F.

4. Test the oil to make sure it will not burn the strips by cooking a small piece of cheese in it. Place 4 to 5 of the strips in the hot oil and fry until golden brown, about 1 minute.

5. Carefully remove the cheese fingers from the oil with a slotted spoon or wire skimmer. Pat dry with paper towels and serve immediately. Continue frying until all of the cheese is used.

Makes 4 servings

NOTE: Mozzarella cheese may be substituted for Fontina cheese in this recipe.

SOUPS

CHICKEN EGG-DROP SOUP WITH CORN

4 cups chicken stock or broth
½ cup water chestnuts, finely
   minced
2½ tablespoons cornstarch
2½ tablespoons cold water
¼ cup green part of scallions, cut
   in ¼-inch pieces
1 egg, lightly beaten
2 cups cooked corn, fresh, canned
   or frozen

1. Bring the chicken stock to a boil in a large saucepan.

2. Add the water chestnuts and simmer for 1 minute.

3. In a small bowl, mix the cornstarch and water until smooth. Stir into the soup and cook, stirring, until the soup thickens.

4. Add the scallions.

5. Turn off the heat. Slowly pour in the beaten egg, stirring gently with chopsticks or a fork.

6. Add the corn, stir and serve at once.

Makes 6 servings

CURRIED CORN SOUP

1 tablespoon unsalted butter
1 large onion, finely chopped
1 tablespoon garlic, finely
    chopped
2 tablespoons curry powder
3 tablespoons all-purpose flour
2 large ripe tomatoes, cored,
    seeded and cut into bite-size
    pieces
4 cups chicken stock or broth
¼ teaspoon Tabasco sauce
2 cups cooked corn, fresh, canned
    or frozen
1 cup plain lowfat yogurt

1. Melt the butter in a saucepan over moderate heat. Add the onion and saute for 2 minutes. Add the garlic and cook for 1 minute more.

2. Stir in the curry powder and flour. Mix in the tomatoes, chicken stock and Tabasco. Simmer for 20 minutes.

3. Puree the soup in a food processor or blender. Return the soup to the pot and bring to a simmer. Add the corn and cook for 1 minute.

4. Off the heat, blend in the yogurt and serve.

Makes 6 servings

COLD YOGURT AND CUCUMBER SOUP

2 cups plain yogurt
1 cucumber, peeled, seeded and
   grated
1 tablespoon white wine vinegar
2 teaspoons fresh mint, chopped
1 teaspoon fresh dill, chopped
2 to 3 sprigs fresh dill, for garnish
   (optional)

1. In a blender or in a bowl with a whisk, combine the yogurt, cucumber, vinegar, mint and chopped dill.

2. Cover and refrigerate for 2 hours.

3. Ladle into bowls and garnish with dill sprigs.

Makes 2 to 3 servings

HOW TO MAKE YOGURT AT HOME

In a very clean saucepan, heat 2 cups of milk to 180°F. Then allow to cool to 110°F. Meanwhile, wash a glass jar with a tight-fitting lid in very hot soapy water. Rinse well with boiling water. Stir 2 tablespoons of store-bought yogurt into the milk. Pour the mixture into the glass jar and seal tight. Put the jar into a preheated 100°F. oven or insulated picnic cooler for 7 hours. Refrigerate the yogurt for 2 hours before using. It will hold in the refrigerator for about 1 week. Save some of the yogurt from this batch to use as a starter for your next batch of yogurt.

SPINACH SOUP WITH PEARS

6 cups chicken stock
1 cup carrots, chopped
1 cup celery, chopped
10 ounces fresh spinach, cleaned
    and stemmed or one 10-ounce
    package frozen spinach,
    thawed and drained
Freshly ground black pepper
1 cup plain yogurt
1 pear, peeled, cored and cut into
    matchstick-size pieces

1. In a large pot, combine the chicken stock, carrots and celery over moderately low heat. Simmer for about 30 minutes.

2. Add the spinach and pepper to taste, cover and cook, for 5 minutes.

3. Puree the mixture in a food processor or blender until smooth. Stir in the yogurt.

4. Return the soup to low heat and cook until just warmed through. Garnish each serving with the pear pieces.

Makes 8 servings

NOTE: Do not bring the soup back to a boil after the yogurt has been added or the yogurt will separate.

BERMUDA VEGETABLE SOUP

2 tablespoons unsalted butter
1 cup celery, chopped
1 cup onion, finely chopped
1 cup green pepper, chopped
1 cup carrots, chopped
1 cup zucchini, chopped
1 cup turnips, finely chopped
1 cup potatoes, chopped
½ cup tomato puree
¼ teaspoon thyme, dried
¼ teaspoon marjoram, dried
Freshly ground black pepper
2 tablespoons Worcestershire
    sauce
3 cups V-8 juice
2 cups water
Fresh parsley, minced,
    for garnish

1. Melt the butter in a large saucepan that is big enough to hold all the ingredients. Add the vegetables and cook, stirring from time to time, for 5 minutes.

2. Pour in the tomato puree and add the thyme, marjoram and pepper. Stir in the Worcestershire sauce, V-8 juice and water. Cook for 5 minutes.

3. Ladle into soup bowls and garnish with parsley before serving.

Makes 10 servings

ONION SOUP LYONNAISE STYLE

2 tablespoons unsalted butter
4 cups onions, thinly sliced
8 cups chicken stock or broth
Salt and freshly ground black
    pepper
1 loaf French or Italian bread,
    3-inch diameter if available
2 cups Gruyere or Swiss cheese,
    shredded

1. Preheat the oven to 400°F.

2. Melt the butter in a large saucepan. Add the onions and saute over moderate heat for 10 to 15 minutes, or until nicely browned.

3. Add the stock and salt and pepper to taste. Bring to a boil, reduce the heat to moderately low and simmer, covered, for 15 minutes.

4. Slice the bread into ¼-inch thick-slices, allowing 2 to 3 slices per serving, depending on the width of the bread. Place the bread slices on a baking sheet and toast in the oven for 3 to 5 minutes, or until golden brown. (Do not turn off the oven.)

5. Place one third of the toast in the bottom of an ovenproof soup tureen or casserole. Sprinkle with ⅔ cup of the cheese. Add half of the remaining toast and cheese. Top with the remaining toast.

6. Pour the soup into the tureen. Sprinkle the remaining cheese on top and bake for about 25 minutes, or the until the cheese is golden brown and bubbling. Serve immediately.

Makes 6 to 8 servings

TUSCAN BEAN SOUP

Two 19-ounce cans cannellini
  beans
3 tablespoons olive oil
2 cloves garlic, crushed
1 medium onion, chopped
1 cup carrots, sliced
1 cup chard or green cabbage,
  chopped
3 tablespoons tomato concentrate
  or tomato paste
3 cups chicken stock or water
Salt and freshly ground black
  pepper
6 slices Italian bread, toasted

1. Drain the beans and puree them in a food mill, food processor or blender.

2. Place the olive oil in a deep saucepan over moderate heat. Add the garlic and onion and saute for 2 minutes. Add the carrots, chard or cabbage and the tomato concentrate and stir. Simmer for 3 minutes.

3. Stir in the pureed beans and the chicken stock and cook for 35 minutes. Season with salt and pepper to taste.

4. Place 1 slice of the toast in the bottom of each bowl and ladle the soup over it.

Makes about 6 servings

BLACK BEAN SOUP

1 pound dried black beans
10 cups chicken stock
4 tablespoons unsalted butter
2 celery ribs, finely chopped
2 medium onions, finely chopped
1 clove garlic, crushed
1½ tablespoons all-purpose flour
1 bay leaf
Salt and freshly ground pepper
½ cup Madeira wine (optional)
Lemon slices, chopped onion,
   chopped tomato and cooked
   rice, for garnish

1. Wash the beans. Place in a large pot and add cold water to cover. Let soak overnight, or boil the beans in 6 to 8 cups of hot water for 2 minutes, then set aside for 1 hour.

2. Drain the beans and place them in a large pot. Add the chicken stock and bring to a boil. Reduce the heat to low and simmer for 1½ hours, adding water if necessary.

3. In another pot, melt the butter over moderate heat. Add the celery, onions and garlic and saute until softened, but not browned, 8 to 10 minutes.

4. Stir in the flour and cook, stirring constantly, for 1 minute.

5. Stir the vegetable mixture into the beans. Add the bay leaf and pepper to taste. Cover and simmer, stirring occasionally, over low heat for 2 to 3 hours. Check occasionally and add water if the beans are not completely covered with liquid.

6. Remove and discard the bay leaf. Add salt to taste. Puree the soup through a food mill, food processor or blender until smooth.

7. Return the soup to the pot and add the Madeira. Reheat the soup and correct the seasoning. Garnish each portion with a lemon slice or serve with chopped onion, chopped tomato and cooked rice.

Makes 6 to 8 servings

THE IMPORTANCE OF REMOVING BAY LEAVES BEFORE SERVING

Bay leaves, which are also called Laurel or Bay Laurel Leaves, add a fragrant and delicate aroma and taste to a dish. They also have a sharp central spine which if eaten whole could become stuck in the digestive tract. They are great for seasoning but not for eating. Remove bay leaves from all recipes before serving.

MANHATTAN CLAM CHOWDER

4 tablespoons unsalted butter
1 cup potato, diced
½ cup celery, diced
½ cup onion, chopped
¼ cup all-purpose flour
6 cups homemade clam broth or
    bottled clam juice
2 tablespoons tomato paste
1 cup canned tomatoes, drained
    and chopped
2 cups cooked fresh or canned
    clams, chopped*
1 teaspoon dried thyme
Salt and freshly ground black
    pepper
Crackers (optional), for serving

1. In a large pot, melt the butter over moderate heat. Add the diced potatoes, celery and onion and saute for 2 minutes. Stir in the flour. Cook for 1 minute, stirring, until thoroughly mixed.

2. Add the clam broth, tomato paste and tomatoes. Mix well. Simmer for 1 hour, stirring occasionally. Add more clam broth or water if necessary.

3. Add the cooked clams and thyme and simmer for 3 minutes. Season with salt and pepper to taste.

4. Serve the chowder with large, plain, white crackers.

Makes 6 servings

*NOTE: If using canned clams, reserve the juice and include in step 2 of the recipe.

FISH & SHELLFISH

BAKED FISH FILLETS IN ORANGE BUTTER

2 pounds white-fleshed fish
   fillets, such as halibut or
   flounder (each fillet should be
   ½-inch thick)
Freshly ground black pepper
1 tablespoon grated lemon zest
1 tablespoon grated orange zest
2 tablespoons scallions, minced
2 tablespoons fresh parsley,
   chopped
2 tablespoons unsalted butter
2 tablespoons fresh lemon juice
2 tablespoons white wine,
   chicken broth or water

1. Preheat the oven to 350°F.

2. Sprinkle the fish fillets with black pepper.

3. Butter a large baking dish and place the fish fillets in a single layer. Sprinkle with the lemon and orange zest. Add the scallions and parsley, and dot with the butter. Pour on the lemon juice and wine.

4. Bake for about 10 minutes, until the fish is opaque and flaky but not dry.

5. Serve the fish with the pan juices.

Makes 4 to 6 servings

FISH FILLETS WITH MUSTARD SAUCE

½ cup mayonnaise
2 tablespoons Dijon-style
   mustard
2 pounds white-fleshed fish
   fillets, such as halibut or
   flounder (each fillet should be
   ½-inch thick)

1. Preheat the broiler.

2. In a small bowl, mix together the mayonnaise and mustard.

3. Arrange the fish in a single layer in a lightly buttered heatproof baking dish. Coat the fish on the top side with ¼-inch-thick layer of the mustard sauce.

4. Broil for 7 minutes; the fillets do not need turning.

Makes 6 servings

FISH COOKERY RULE
1. Measure the fish at its thickest point.
2. Allow 10 minutes of cooking time per inch of thickness.
3. Double the cooking time for frozen fish.
4. Add an extra 5 minutes for fish cooking in foil or sauce.

BLACKENED REDFISH

2 tablespoons (total) mixed
   spices: use salt, black pepper,
   Cayenne pepper, oregano
   and thyme
4 tablespoons unsalted butter
One 6-ounce boneless, skinless
   fillet of redfish, tile fish or
   salmon

1. Place a cast-iron skillet over high heat and preheat until the surface of the pan is as hot as possible, about 10 minutes.

2. Melt the butter in a skillet or saute pan. Spread the spice mixture on a flat dish. Dip both sides of the fish fillet into the melted butter and then into the mixed spices.

3. Pan fry the fish for 2 minutes on each side.

Makes 1 serving

NOTE: The trick to this dish is to get the cast-iron skillet so hot that the surface of the fish is almost seared by its first contact with the pan. The heat can be generated on top of a normal stove or it can be prepared by placing the pan directly on top of ash-covered coals in an outdoor barbecue grill.

SAUTEED FLOUNDER WITH SHRIMP

2 pounds flounder fillets, cut into
   a total of 4 pieces, each ½-inch
   thick
2 eggs, beaten
¼ cup dry bread crumbs
5 tablespoons unsalted butter
2 tablespoons vegetable oil
8 large shrimps, shelled and
   deveined

1. Lightly coat the flounder with the flour (shaking off any excess), then dip the fish into the eggs and finally into the bread crumbs.

2. Melt 2 tablespoons of the butter with the vegetable oil in a saute pan over moderate heat. When almost smoking, add the flounder and saute for 2 to 3 minutes on each side, until nicely browned. Remove the fillets to a serving dish.

3. Heat the remaining 3 tablespoons butter in the same pan until it begins to brown. Saute the shrimp for 2 minutes and place 2 of the cooked shrimp on top of each fillet. Pour the butter sauce over the shrimp and fish and serve.

Makes 4 servings

LOUISIANA SHRIMP & CRABMEAT SAUTE

2 tablespoons unsalted butter
¼ cup scallions, chopped
1 clove garlic, minced
1 cup shrimp, peeled and
    deveined
½ teaspoon freshly ground black
    pepper
¼ teaspoon Cayenne pepper
½ teaspoon dried oregano
½ teaspoon dried thyme
2 tablespoons Dijon-style
    mustard
½ cup mushrooms, sliced
1 cup cooked lump crabmeat
⅓ cup fish stock, white wine or
    water
4 cups cooked rice, for serving

1. Melt the butter in a saute pan over moderate heat. Add the scallions and garlic and cook for 1 minute. Add the shrimp and cook until they start to curl and turn pink, about 2 minutes.

2. Add the spices and herbs and saute for 30 seconds. Stir in the mustard and saute for 30 seconds. Add the mushrooms and saute for 30 seconds. Add the crabmeat and saute for 30 seconds. Stir in the stock and cook for 1 minute.

3. Serve over cooked rice.

Makes 4 servings

CRABMEAT IMPERIAL

1½ pounds cooked lump
  crabmeat
½ cup green pepper, diced
2 tablespoons pimiento, diced
¼ cup scallions, diced
1 egg yolk
1 tablespoon Worcestershire
  sauce
Dash of Tabasco sauce
1 tablespoon Dijon-style mustard
6 tablespoons mayonnaise

1. Preheat the oven to 350°F.

2. In a mixing bowl, gently stir together the lump crabmeat, green pepper, pimiento, scallions, egg yolk, Worcestershire sauce, Tabasco, mustard and 3 tablespoons of the mayonnaise.

3. Divide the mixture among 6 small ramekins or custard cups or place in one large baking dish. Spread the remaining 3 tablespoons mayonnaise on top and bake for 12 minutes, or until the top is nicely browned.

Makes 6 servings

NOTE: You can do all the preparation for this dish in advance and keep the crabmeat mixture in a covered bowl for 24 hours in the refrigerator. Cook it just before serving.

SALMON LOAF

1 cup cooked whole-grain (brown)
    rice
One 15-ounce can salmon,
    drained
1 cup plain dry bread crumbs
½ cup skim milk
2 eggs
1 tablespoon fresh parsley,
    chopped
1 tablespoon unsalted butter
2 tablespoons fresh lemon juice
1 tablespoon fresh dill, chopped
    (optional)
Salt and freshly ground black
    pepper
Sliced cucumbers, for garnish

1. Cook the rice.

2. Preheat the oven to 375°F.

3. In a bowl, combine all of the ingredients except for the sliced cucumbers and shape into a long loaf. Butter a 9 x 5 x 3-inch loaf pan and place the salmon loaf in it. Bake for 45 minutes.

4. Unmold and serve, surrounded by sliced cucumbers.

Makes 6 servings

WHOLE-GRAIN (OR BROWN) RICE AND NUTRITION
White rice is made by milling off the bran layer of whole-grain rice. Whole-grain (or brown) rice has the bran layer intact, which results in a rice with more protein, calcium, phosphorus, potassium, niacin and vitamin E.

POULTRY

GRILLED CHICKEN WITH MUSTARD SAUCE

1 teaspoon unsalted butter
4 boneless skinless chicken
   breasts, split, fat removed and
   pounded lightly
2 tablespoons Dijon-style
   mustard
1 tablespoon plus 1 teaspoon
   mayonnaise
1 tablespoon plain yogurt

1. Preheat the broiler.

2. Butter the bottom of a heatproof baking dish that will hold the chicken breasts in a single layer.

3. Place the chicken breasts, skinned side up, in the pan.

4. Blend together the mustard, mayonnaise and yogurt. Spread the mixture over the chicken breasts.

5. Place the baking dish about 6 inches below your heating element and cook for 15 minutes.

Makes 8 servings

MOROCCAN-STYLE BROILED CHICKEN

3 scallions, white part only,
  chopped
1 clove garlic, chopped
1 tablespoon fresh coriander,
  coarsely chopped
1 tablespoon fresh parsley,
  coarsely chopped
1 teaspoon salt
1½ teaspoons paprika (sweet
  variety, if available)
Pinch of Cayenne pepper
1½ teaspoons ground cumin
4 tablespoons unsalted butter,
  at room temperature
One 4-pound broiling-frying
  chicken, quartered

1. In a bowl, mix together the scallions, garlic, herbs, salt and spices. Blend with the butter to make a paste.

2. Rub the paste over the chicken pieces, inside and out, reserving any extra paste for basting. Let stand for 1 hour.

3. Burn the charcoal in an outdoor grill or preheat the broiler.

4. If using a grill, arrange the chicken pieces skin-side up over the coals. If broiling, arrange chicken, skin-side down, in a baking pan and place under the broiler. Cook for 5 minutes, turn and baste with any extra paste or the juices in the roasting pan. Continue turning and basting every 5 minutes, until the chicken is cooked through.

Makes 4 servings

PECAN BREADED CHICKEN

4 whole boneless, skinless
   chicken breasts, split
Freshly ground black pepper
6 tablespoons unsalted butter
¼ cup plus 2 tablespoons Dijon-
   style mustard
2 cups pecans, finely ground
2 cups sour cream

1. Preheat the oven to 400°F.

2. Flatten the chicken breasts with a meat pounder and lightly pepper them.

3. In a saucepan, melt the butter and then remove the pan from the heat. Whisk in ¼ cup of the mustard.

4. Dip the chicken into the butter and mustard mixture and then into the ground pecans.

5. Lightly butter a baking pan and place the chicken breasts in it. (At this point you may refrigerate the chicken breasts for up to 24 hours or cook them.)

6. Place the pan in the oven and bake for about 15 minutes, until golden. Remove the chicken from the pan.

7. Pour the pan drippings into a bowl, add the sour cream and the remaining 2 tablespoons mustard and mix thoroughly.

8. Place 2 tablespoons of the sour cream and mustard mixture on each dinner plate and cover with a chicken breast.

Makes 8 servings

CHICKEN GRUYERE

Batter:
2½ cups Gruyere cheese,
   finely shredded
2 eggs
⅓ cup milk
⅓ cup light cream
1 tablespoon all-purpose flour
Salt and freshly ground black
   pepper
Pinch of nutmeg

Chicken:
1 cup all-purpose flour
3 whole boneless, skinless
   chicken breasts, split and
   flattened
1 teaspoon vegetable oil, for the
   skillet

1. Preheat the oven to 350°F.

2. In a bowl, combine all of the batter ingredients and mix well.

3. Lightly dredge the chicken breasts in the flour. Dip the floured chicken in the batter and coat evenly.

4. Using a nonstick skillet with a heatproof handle, lightly coat the bottom with the oil. Add the chicken breasts and saute until nicely browned on one side. Turn the chicken breasts and bake for 10 minutes, until browned and cooked through.

Makes 6 servings

YOGURT BAKED CHICKEN

One 2½ to 3-pound frying
  chicken, cut into 6 to 8 pieces
½ cup dry bread crumbs
¼ teaspoon salt
1 teaspoon garlic, finely minced
½ teaspoon paprika
¼ teaspoon curry powder
¼ teaspoon freshly ground black
  pepper
½ cup plain yogurt

1. Preheat the oven to 350°F. Line a shallow baking pan with heavy-duty aluminum foil and grease the foil lightly.

2. Rinse the chicken pieces and pat them dry. Remove the skin, if desired.

3. In a shallow plate, combine the bread crumbs, salt, garlic, paprika, curry powder and black pepper.

4. Place the yogurt in a shallow dish and lightly coat the chicken pieces in it. Dredge the pieces in the seasoned crumbs.

5. Arrange the chicken in the prepared pan and bake for 45 minutes, until cooked through.

6. Serve hot, or, if made ahead of time, serve cold. It's perfect for a picnic, eaten out of hand, like fried chicken.

Makes 4 servings

CHICKEN WITH FORTY GLOVES OF GARLIC

2 frying chickens, quartered
40 cloves garlic
4 celery ribs
⅔ cup olive oil
6 sprigs parsley
1 tablespoon dried tarragon
1 teaspoon salt
¼ teaspoon freshly ground black
    pepper
Dash of nutmeg

1. Preheat the oven to 375°F.

2. Peel the garlic, leaving the cloves whole. Thinly slice the celery.

3. Put the oil into a large, heavy baking pan that will hold the chicken pieces in one layer. Add the celery, parsley and tarragon. Arrange the chicken pieces on top and sprinkle with the salt, pepper and nutmeg. Turn the chicken several times so all surfaces are coated with oil. Toss in the garlic. Cover with heavy-duty aluminum foil, making sure that the edges are tightly sealed.

4. Bake for 1½ hours, without removing the foil.

5. Remove the foil and bake for an additional 15 minutes, or until browned. Serve the chicken with the garlic.

Makes 4 to 6 servings

CHICKEN OR TURKEY CHILI

1 teaspoon vegetable oil
2 medium onions, diced
2 cloves garlic, minced
One 32-ounce can Italian plum
   tomatoes, drained
Pinch of Cayenne pepper
3 to 5 drops Tabasco sauce
3 tablespoons chili powder
3 cups cooked chicken or turkey,
   diced
1 cup cooked corn, fresh, canned
   or frozen
One 15-ounce can red kidney
   beans, drained and rinsed
Cooked rice (optional),
   for serving

1. Coat a medium saucepan with the vegetable oil and place over moderate heat. Add the onions and cook until translucent. Add the garlic and cook for about 2 minutes, without browning the garlic or onions.

2. Add the tomatoes, Cayenne, Tabasco, and chili powder and cook for 3 minutes, until heated through.

3. Mix in the cooked chicken or turkey, corn and kidney beans and heat thoroughly. Serve over rice.

Makes 6 servings

CALCUTTA CHICKEN CURRY SAUCE

2 tablespoons unsalted butter
1 onion, chopped
1 large clove garlic, minced
3 tablespoons curry powder
1 large green apple, cored,
    seeded and diced
2 tablespoons cucumber, peeled
    and diced
2 tablespoons pimiento, chopped
2 large carrots, chopped
2 cups chicken stock
½ cup coconut cream
Cooked chicken, for serving

1. In a large saucepan, melt the butter over moderate heat. Add the onions and garlic and saute until the onion is limp, about 3 minutes. Stir in the curry powder and cook for 2 more minutes.

2. Add the apple and stir. Add the cucumber, pimiento and carrots and cook for 1 minute. Add the chicken stock and bring to a boil. Cook for 5 minutes.

3. Puree the curry sauce in a food mill, food processor or blender and return the sauce to the pan.

4. Stir in the coconut milk and reheat over low heat.

5. Serve over cooked chicken.

Makes 4 servings

MEAT

DANISH MEATBALLS

½ pound ground veal, ground
   twice
½ pound ground pork, ground
   twice
1 onion, finely chopped
1 cup dry bread crumbs
4 eggs
1½ cups club soda or seltzer
4 tablespoons unsalted butter
¼ cup vegetable oil

1. In a mixing bowl, combine the veal, pork, onion, bread crumbs and eggs.

2. Slowly add the club soda and mix until thoroughly combined.

3. Shape the meat into small 1-inch balls.

4. In a skillet or saute pan, melt the butter with the vegetable oil over moderate heat. Fry the meatballs until lightly crusted on all sides.

Makes 4 servings

ALAMO BURGERS

1 pound ground beef chuck
¼ cup taco sauce
4 pita breads
Refried beans, warmed
½ head iceberg lettuce, finely
  sliced
1 cup cheddar or Monterey Jack
  cheese, shredded

1. Burn charcoals in an outdoor grill or preheat the broiler.

2. In a bowl, mix the beef with the taco sauce.

3. Shape the meat into four patties and grill or broil to the desired point of doneness.

4. Slice 1 inch off one side of each pita bread and open the pocket. Coat one side of the inside of the pita with some of the warm refried beans.

5. Put the burger into the pita pocket and stuff with lettuce and cheese.

Makes 4 servings

HAMBURGER TIPS:

Most people prefer hamburgers made with a mixture of beef that is 75 percent meat and 25 percent fat. Beef chuck has this ratio naturally and is, therefore, ideal as a cut for hamburgers.

Handle the meat as little as possible during the preparation. The more ground meat is handled, the more juice is lost. For the same reason, a hamburger should not be pressed down to the cooking surface. The pressure pushes out the meat's natural juices.

PEPPER STEAK

⅓ cup vegetable oil
2 pounds top round steak,
    trimmed of all fat and cut into
    ½-inch strips
Salt and freshly ground black
    pepper
1 medium onion, chopped
2 large garlic cloves, chopped
3 medium red peppers, cored,
    seeded and cut into strips
3 medium green peppers, cored,
    seeded and cut into strips
2 cups fresh mushrooms, sliced
2 cups beef stock
1 tablespoon Worcestershire
    sauce
3 tablespoons cornstarch
½ cup water
¼ cup soy sauce
8 cups cooked rice,
    for serving

1. In a skillet, warm the oil over moderate heat. Add the steak strips, and cook until lightly browned.

2. Season with salt and pepper to taste and stir in the onion, garlic, peppers and mushrooms. Saute, stirring often, for 5 minutes, or until the vegetables are tender. Add the beef stock and Worcestershire sauce and cook for 2 minutes more.

3. In a small bowl, stir together the cornstarch and water.

4. Add the cornstarch mixture and soy sauce to the steak and cook for 2 minutes, stirring constantly, until thickened. Serve with rice.

Makes 8 servings

STEAK WITH MUSTARD CREAM SAUCE

Four 6-ounce boneless shell
   steaks (New York strip),
   trimmed of all fat
1 teaspoon freshly ground black
   pepper
3 tablespoons unsalted butter
½ cup red wine
4 tablespoons coarse-grain
   mustard
1½ cups heavy cream

1. Preheat the oven to 180°F.

2. Sprinkle both sides of each steak with the pepper. Melt the butter over moderately high heat in a large heavy skillet that will hold all the steaks in a single layer. Saute the steaks for 4 minutes on each side. Using tongs, remove the steaks to a heatproof serving platter and keep them warm in the oven.

3. Add the red wine to the skillet and cook over high heat, scraping up the browned bits that cling to the bottom of the pan.

4. Add the mustard and cook, stirring for about 1 minute. Add the cream and reduce the heat to low. Simmer for 4 minutes until the sauce is thick enough to coat the back of a spoon.

5. Remove the steaks from the oven and pour the sauce over them. Serve immediately.

Makes 6 servings

ORIENTAL IMPERIAL STEAK

½ cup safflower oil
6 to 8 ounces filet of beef,
   trimmed of all fat and cut into
   cubes
Dash of sherry wine
8 whole dried Chinese
   mushrooms, soaked and sliced
   lengthwise
8 snow peas, cut into ½-inch
   pieces
½ cup bamboo shoots, drained
   and sliced
½ cup sliced water chestnuts
1 small head bok choy (Chinese
   cabbage), shredded
1 cup chicken stock
1 tablespoon oyster sauce
1 tablespoon cornstarch dissolved
   in 2 tablespoons cold water

1. In a wok or deep skillet, heat ¼ cup of the oil until almost smoking. Add the beef cubes and cook stirring, for 2 minutes until browned. Add the sherry and cook, stirring for 2 minutes more. Remove the beef and set aside.

2. Add the remaining ¼ cup oil and all of the vegetables. Stir fry for 2 minutes.

3. Add the chicken stock, cover and cook for 2 minutes.

4. Add the oyster sauce and the cornstarch and water mixture and cook for 2 minutes more.

5. Return the steak to the pan and cook until just heated through. Serve immediately.

Makes 4 servings

SOY SAUCE GINGER BEEF

2 pounds boneless beef shank,
   shin or chuck, trimmed of
   all fat
3 tablespoons peanut oil
2 scallions, white and green
   parts, cut into 1-inch lengths
½ cup dry sherry
3 tablespoons dark soy sauce
1 tablespoon sugar
2 slices fresh ginger, each about
   ¼-inch thick
1 cup cold water

1. Cut the beef into 1-inch cubes.

2. Place 2 tablespoons of the oil in a large skillet over high heat. Add half of the beef cubes and stir-fry until seared on all sides. Remove the meat cubes and repeat with the remaining 1 tablespoon oil and the beef.

3. Return the beef to the skillet. Add the scallions, sherry, soy sauce, sugar and ginger and cook, stirring, over high heat. Add the water and bring to a boil. Cover, reduce the heat to moderately low and cook, stirring occasionally, for 1 hour, or until the meat is tender. There should be about ½ cup of liquid left. If there is more, increase the heat to high, uncover the pan and cook for 5 minutes more.

Makes 4 to 6 servings

VEAL SALTIMBOCCA

1½ pounds boneless veal
   scallopine, cut into thin slices*
½ cup all-purpose flour
Two 10-ounce packages frozen
   leaf spinach, or 2 pounds fresh
   spinach
2 tablespoons unsalted butter
½ cup vegetable oil
½ pound prosciutto Italian-style
   cured ham, thinly sliced
½ teaspoon dried sage
2 teaspoons fresh parsley, finely
   chopped
Salt and freshly ground black
   pepper
2 hard-cooked eggs, peeled and
   sliced crosswise into rounds
   (optional)

1. Place the sliced veal between 2 sheets of waxed paper and pound them into thin scallops with a mallet or the flat side of a cleaver. Lightly dust the veal scallops with flour.

2. Cook the frozen spinach according to package directions. Drain and toss with the butter. (If fresh spinach is used, wash very well in cold running water and remove the stems. Cook in a covered pan in just the water that clings to the leaves after washing. Cook about 5 minutes, or just until tender. Drain and stir in the butter.) Make a bed of the hot spinach on a large platter.

3. Heat half the oil in a large skillet. Place as many veal scallops in the pan as will fit without crowding. Cook until lightly golden on both sides. Remove the veal from the pan and drain on paper towels. Repeat with the remaining veal, adding more oil as needed.

4. Cut the prosciutto slices to approximately the size of the veal scallops.

5. Sprinkle each veal scallop with the sage, parsley and 2 turns of the pepper mill. Lay slices of prosciutto on each veal slice.

6. Arrange the veal on top of the spinach. Place a slice of egg, if used, on each scallop and spoon the pan juices over all.

Makes 4 servings

*NOTE: Boneless and skinless chicken breasts may be substituted for the veal in this recipe.

BUTTERFLIED LEG OF LAMB

1 leg of lamb, boned and
    butterflied (ask your butcher to
    do this)
2 cloves garlic, minced
1 tablespoon dried thyme,
    crushed
1 tablespoon dried rosemary,
    crushed
2 tablespoons coarse-grain
    mustard
¼ cup vegetable oil
Salt and freshly ground black
    pepper

1. Burn the coals in an outdoor grill or preheat the broiler.

2. Spread out the lamb on a board and rub it well with the garlic, thyme and rosemary.

3. In a small bowl, combine the mustard and oil.

4. Place the lamb on a broiling pan or rack and broil 4 to 5 inches from the heat, basting occasionally with the mustard sauce and turning once or twice, for 40 to 50 minutes, depending on the desired degree of doneness. Internal temperatures for lamb can be checked with an instant reading meat thermometer: Rare at 140°F., Medium at 150°F., Well at 160°F.

5. Remove the lamb to a cutting board and cut on the diagonal into ¼-inch slices.

Makes 10 to 12 servings

PORK CHOPS IN COUNTRY-STYLE MUSTARD SAUCE

4 tablespoons unsalted butter
6 loin pork chops, cut 1¼-inches
    thick
Salt and freshly ground black
    pepper
3 tablespoons shallots or
    scallions, minced
½ cup dry white wine
2 cups heavy cream
½ cup coarse-grain mustard

1. In a heavy skillet large enough to hold the pork chops in one layer, melt 2 tablespoons of butter over moderately high heat until foamy. Add the pork chops and brown well on both sides. (If you do not have a pan large enough to prepare all the chops at one time, they can be prepared in smaller batches.)

2. Season with salt and pepper to taste. Reduce the heat to low, cover and cook for 15 minutes. Transfer the chops to a platter; set aside and keep warm.

3. Pour off the fat from the skillet. Increase the heat to moderate, add the remaining 2 tablespoons of butter and the shallots and saute for 30 seconds. Increase the heat to high, stir in the wine and cook, scraping up the brown bits that cling to the bottom of the pan, until the liquid is syrupy and reduced by half, about 2 minutes. Blend in the cream and the mustard and cook, stirring, for 2 minute more. Do not allow the sauce to boil.

4. Pour the sauce over the pork chops and serve.

Makes 6 servings

STUFFED PORK CHOPS

NOTE: For this recipe use either rib or loin chops and have them cut thick. Ask your butcher to cut a pocket in each—or do it yourself, following the directions below.

6 rib or loin pork chops, 1 to 1½—
    inches thick, trimmed of all fat
4 tablespoons unsalted butter
1 medium onion, finely chopped
1 celery rib, finely chopped
1 garlic clove, finely minced
3 large fresh mushrooms, finely
    chopped
1 teaspoon dried thyme or
    rosemary
1 cup dry bread crumbs
½ cup fresh parsley, chopped
½ teaspoon salt
½ teaspoon freshly ground
    pepper
4 tablespoons vegetable oil
Boiling water
1 cup brown sauce or gravy or 3
    tablespoons all-purpose flour
    and 1 cup beef broth or
    bouillon

1. With a sharp knife, cut a 2½-inch pocket in the fat-edged side of each pork chop that reaches deep into the meat, until the tip of the knife touches the bone. Set aside.

2. Prepare the stuffing: Melt the butter in a medium skillet over moderate heat. Add the onion, celery, garlic, mushrooms and thyme. Cook, stirring, until the vegetables are softened, about 5 minutes. Stir in the bread crumbs, parsley, and salt and pepper. Blend thoroughly, the mixture should be fairly dry.

3. Using a teaspoon, fill the pocket in each chop with the prepared stuffing, dividing the mixture evenly. As each chop is stuffed, press the cut edges together to enclose the stuffing and secure the pocket with small skewers or wooden toothpicks.

4. Choose a skillet with a tight-fitting lid that is large enough to hold all the chops in a single layer. Warm the oil over moderately high heat. Add the stuffed chops and brown well on one side.

5. Carefully turn the chops, taking care not to disturb the stuffing and brown the second side.

6. Add just enough boiling water to cover the bottom of the skillet. Cover tightly, reduce the heat to low and simmer for 25 minutes, adding additional water if necessary.

7. Carefully turn the chops, replace the lid and simmer for 10 to 20 minutes longer, depending on the thickness of the chops. Chops should be tender but not dry. When cooked, transfer to a hot platter and keep warm.

8. With a large spoon, skim off any fat from the pan juices. Add the brown sauce to the pan and heat, stirring occasionally, just to a boil. Or, stir the flour into the pan juices, blend well and cook for several minutes. Add broth and stir over moderately high heat until the mixture thickens. Taste and correct seasonings; spoon the sauce over the chops. Remove the skewers or toothpicks and serve.

Makes 6 servings

PASTA & RICE

SPAGHETTI CARBONARA

½ pound spaghetti
4 tablespoons unsalted butter
½ cup cooked bacon, chopped
½ cup prosciutto Italian style
    cured ham, thinly sliced
    and chopped
2 egg yolks
½ cup heavy cream
Freshly ground black pepper
¼ cup Parmesan cheese, freshly
    grated
Additional freshly grated
    Parmesan cheese, for garnish

1. Cook the spaghetti in 4 quarts of salted boiling water until tender but still firm to the bite.

2. Meanwhile, melt the butter in a large saute pan or skillet over moderate heat. Add the bacon and prosciutto and saute for 2 minutes.

3. In a mixing bowl, stir together the egg yolks, heavy cream, black pepper to taste and the Parmesan cheese.

4. Drain the spaghetti and add to the bacon and prosciutto. Mix well and pour in the cream mixture. Cook, tossing, for 1 minute until the pasta is well coated with the sauce. Season to taste with black pepper.

5. Serve hot, with Parmesan cheese on top.

Makes 2 servings

PASTA WITH TOMATO AND CREAM SAUCE

¼ pound unsalted butter
3 tablespoons onion, finely
   chopped
3 tablespoons carrot, finely
   chopped
3 tablespoons celery, finely
   chopped
2½ cups canned Italian plum
   tomatoes, with their juice
¼ teaspoon sugar
Salt
1 pound pasta
½ cup heavy cream

1. In a large saucepan, melt the butter over moderate heat.
Add the onion, carrot and celery and saute for 3 minutes. Stir
in the tomatoes, sugar and salt to taste. Reduce the heat to low
and simmer, stirring from time to time, for 1 hour.

2. In a large pot of salted boiling water, cook the pasta until
tender but still firm to the bite.

3. Meanwhile, puree the tomato sauce in a food mill, food
processor or blender. Return the sauce to the saucepan and
bring to a simmer. Add the heavy cream and cook, stirring, for
1 minute more.

4. Drain the pasta and turn into a serving bowl. Add the
tomato and cream sauce and toss well. Serve immediately.

Makes 6 servings

TORTELLINI SALAD

Vinaigrette:
2 tablespoons Dijon-style
    mustard
⅓ cup red wine vinegar
¾ cup olive oil
2 cloves garlic, finely minced
Salt and freshly ground black
    pepper

Salad:
1 pound meat or cheese-filled
    tortellini, cooked and cooled
1 cup broccoli flowerets,
    blanched
⅓ cup red onion, finely chopped
1 red pepper, finely chopped
½ cup fresh parsley, finely
    chopped
1 cup pitted black olives
    (optional)
Freshly grated Parmesan cheese
    (optional), for serving

1. Make the vinaigrette. In a mixing bowl, whisk together the mustard, vinegar, olive oil, garlic, and salt and pepper to taste.

2. Place the cooked tortellini in a serving bowl and toss with the vinaigrette dressing. Add the broccoli, onion, red pepper, parsley and olives and toss. Cover and refrigerate.

3. Remove from the refrigerator and allow to come to room temperature. Serve with grated Parmesan cheese.

Makes 4 servings

SPRING PASTA

1 pound spaghetti
3 tablespoons olive oil
1 cup cooked ham, cut into thin
    slivers, about 2-inches long
1 cup zucchini, cut into thin
    slivers, about 2-inches long
1 cup canned Italian plum
    tomatoes, crushed
1 tablespoon fresh basil,
    chopped or 1 teaspoon dried
    sweet basil
Salt and freshly ground black
    pepper
Freshly grated Parmesan cheese,
    for serving

1. In a large pot of salted boiling water, cook the spaghetti until tender but still firm to the bite. Drain thoroughly in a colander.

2. Meanwhile, in a saucepan, combine the olive oil, ham, zucchini, tomatoes and basil over moderate heat. Season with salt and pepper to taste, and cook stirring from time to time, for 7 minutes.

3. Turn the spaghetti into a large serving bowl. Add the sauce and toss to combine. Serve with Parmesan cheese.

Makes 4 servings

ROMAN STREET PASTA

5 tablespoons olive oil
2 cloves garlic, minced
2 to 3 slices Italian bread, cut into
    1/4-inch cubes (about 1 cup)
8 anchovy fillets, finely chopped
4½ cups Italian plum tomatoes,
    drained and pureed through a
    food mill or a coarse sieve
8 pitted black olives, sliced
1 teaspoon capers
1 tablespoon fresh basil,
    chopped or 1 teaspoon dried
    sweet basil
1/4 teaspoon hot red pepper flakes
1 pound linguine or spaghettini

1. In a large saucepan, heat 2 tablespoons of the oil over moderate heat and saute the garlic and the bread cubes until the bread is crisp. Remove the croutons from the pan and set aside.

2. Add the remaining 3 tablespoons oil to the saucepan and stir in the anchovies. Add the tomatoes and simmer for 10 minutes.

3. Stir in the olives, capers, basil and red pepper flakes. Simmer, uncovered, over low heat for 20 minutes, or until thickened.

4. Meanwhile, in a large pot of salted boiling water, cook the linguine until tender but still firm to the bite. Drain well.

5. Serve the sauce over the linguine and top with the croutons.

Makes 4 to 6 servings

RICOTTA, SPINACH AND NOODLE PUDDING

6 ounces (about 3 cups) medium-
    size egg noodles
4 tablespoons unsalted butter
¾ cup onion, finely chopped
½ teaspoon garlic, finely minced
One 10-ounce package frozen
    chopped spinach, partially
    thawed
One 15-ounce container whole-
    milk ricotta cheese
1 teaspoon salt
¼ teaspoon freshly ground black
    pepper
¼ cup fine, dry bread crumbs

1. Preheat the oven to 375°F. Butter a 1½-quart deep baking
dish or souffle dish.

2. In a pot of salted boiling water, cook the noodles until not
quite tender.

3. Meanwhile, melt 1 tablespoon of the butter in a large
skillet over moderate heat. Add the onions and garlic and cook
until softened, 3 to 5 minutes.

4. Drain the noddles. Turn into a large saucepan and toss
with 2 tablespoons of the butter. Set aside.

5. Add the spinach to the onions and garlic and cook, covered,
over moderate heat for 5 minutes. Uncover and cook briefly to
evaporate most of the liquid.

6. Add the onion-spinach mixture to the noodles. Stir in the
ricotta, salt and pepper and mix well. Scoop the mixture into
the prepared baking dish.

7. In a small skillet, melt the remaining 1 tablespoon butter
and stir in the bread crumbs. Sprinkle the crumbs evenly over
the noodle mixture. Bake for 35 to 40 minutes, until the cheese
is melted and the crumbs are lightly browned. Serve hot.

Makes 3 to 4 main-course servings or 6 to 8 side dishes

MACARONI WITH HAM AND CHEESE

3 tablespoons unsalted butter
2 shallots, finely minced
3 tablespoons all-purpose flour
2 cups milk
Salt and freshly ground black
    pepper
2 cups cooked ham, cut into
    ¼-inch cubes
1 cup Jarlsberg cheese, shredded
Dash of Tabasco sauce (optional)
½ pound elbow macaroni
Butter and dry bread crumbs, for
    topping

1. Preheat the oven to 375°F. Butter a 6 to 8-cup baking pan, sprinkle with bread crumbs and set aside.

2. In a saucepan, melt the butter; add the shallots and cook a few minutes to soften. Add the flour, stir and cook for 2 minutes. Add the milk, stirring with a whisk, and cook until thickened.

3. Add the salt and pepper to taste, and stir. Fold in the ham and cheese, add Tabasco to taste and set aside.

4. In a large pot of salted boiling water, cook the macaroni until tender but still firm to the bite. Drain well and return to the pot. Add the sauce and mix well.

5. Turn the mixture into the prepared pan, sprinkle with the bread crumbs and dot lightly with butter.

6. Cover with foil and bake for 30 minutes. Uncover, raise the heat to 425°F. and bake about 10 minutes longer, or until golden and bubbling.

Makes 2 servings

BACON FRIED RICE

3 cups cold cooked rice
½ pound bacon, cut into ½-inch
   pieces
3 tablespoons vegetable oil
2 eggs, beaten
1½ tablespoons soy sauce
½ cup scallions, greens only,
   coarsely chopped

1. Cook the rice at least several hours ahead (or the day before) and refrigerate. It must be completely cold to be used for fried rice.

2. Fry the bacon until crisp and drain on paper towels.

3. Heat 1 tablespoon of the oil in a wok or large skillet. Add the eggs and cook, stirring, just until firm. Remove from the pan and reserve.

4. Heat the remaining 2 tablespoons oil in the pan and add the rice. Mix well. Add the soy sauce and mix well. Mix the eggs into the rice, breaking them into smaller pieces as you stir. Add the scallions and bacon. Mix again to combine and serve.

Makes 4 servings

NOTE: This dish can be kept in a casserole in the oven at 140°F. for about 40 minutes without drying out. It makes a good dish to serve with a main course that needs last-minute preparation.

TURMERIC RICE

2 tablespoons vegetable oil
1 medium onion, minced
1 cup whole-grain (brown) rice
1 tablespoon turmeric
2 cups chicken stock or broth

1. Combine the oil and onion in a saucepan and cook over moderate heat until the onion is translucent and milky in color, about 5 minutes.

2. Add the rice and turmeric and mix together.

3. Add the stock. Bring to a boil over high heat, reduce the heat to low and stir with a fork. Cover and cook for 45 minutes, without removing the cover during the cooking time. Fluff the rice with a fork.

Makes 4 servings

NOTE: Turmeric is a spice in the ginger family which is used in making curry powder and mustard. In this dish, it imparts a warm, yellow color and mild Oriental flavor to the rice.

This dish can also be prepared with polished or white rice, though you will be losing the superior nutritive value of the whole grain. Adjust the recipe in step 3, using the amount of liquid and cooking time recommended on the white rice package.

A fork is suggested for fluffing the rice after it is cooked rather than a spoon. Spoons tend to compress the rice and make it lump together.

VEGETABLES

BERMUDA ONIONS BRAISED WITH MADEIRA

2 tablespoons olive oil
2 tablespoons unsalted butter
4 large Bermuda onions, sliced
    1-inch thick
1 teaspoon salt
½ teaspoon freshly ground
    pepper
¼ cup beef stock or broth
¼ cup Madeira wine

1. Melt the oil and butter in a heavy saute pan over high heat.

2. Add the onions and sear on one side for 2 minutes.

3. Turn the onions and season with the salt and pepper. Add the stock, cover and reduce the heat to low. Simmer for 10 minutes, or just until tender.

4. Add the Madeira and cook until the sauce is slightly reduced.

Makes 4 servings

BRAISED RED CABBAGE

2 heads red cabbage (about
   4 pounds)
3 tablespoons vegetable oil
2 cups onions, sliced
½ cup red wine vinegar
¾ cup water
½ tablespoon caraway seeds
¼ cup brown sugar

1. Cut out the cores of the cabbages and discard. Cut the cabbages into bite-size pieces.

2. In a large saucepan or stockpot, heat the vegetable oil over moderate heat and cook the onions for 2 minutes.

3. Add the cabbage, cover, and cook for 5 minutes.

4. Add the vinegar, water, caraway seeds and brown sugar and cook the cabbage, covered, for 45 minutes, or until tender.

Makes 8 servings

NOTE: To braise a food is to cook it by surrounding it with moist heat. This is done by putting a small amount of moisture under the food and heating it in a tightly closed pot. It is a good cooking method because it tends to hold in a food's nutrients, and cabbage is filled with healthy elements including vitamin C and fiber.

AMISH CARROTS

6 carrots, scrubbed or peeled
½ cup mayonnaise
2 tablespoons prepared white
    horseradish
¼ cup water
Freshly ground black pepper
¼ cup sliced almonds

1. Preheat the oven to 350°F.

2. Cut the carrots into strips and steam for 8 minutes.

3. While the carrots are steaming, mix together the mayonnaise, horseradish and water.

4. Turn the carrots into a baking dish and pour in the mayonnaise mixture to coat evenly. Add a few grinds of pepper and sprinkle the sliced almonds over the top.

5. Bake for 10 minutes, until bubbly, and serve immediately.

Makes 4 servings

CARROTS AND NUTRITION

Carrots contain carotene which is changed by our liver into vitamin A. Vitamin A prevents night blindness (or improves night vision), promotes and is necessary for healthy skin and mucous membranes and promotes the proper functioning of your body's immune system. It also may be helpful in preventing certain types of cancer, such as lung and bladder cancer.

BROCCOLI PUREE

2 bunches broccoli
¼ cup heavy cream
2 tablespoons unsalted butter
¼ teaspoon ground nutmeg
1 teaspoon fresh lemon juice

1. Using a vegetable peeler, peel away the tough skin from the broccoli stems. Cut off the flowerets. Cut the stems crosswise into ½-inch rounds.

2. Steam the stems and flowerets for 5 minutes.

3. Place the broccoli in a food mill or food processor. Add the heavy cream, butter, nutmeg and lemon juice and blend until smooth.

Makes 4 servings

BROCCOLI AND NUTRITION
Broccoli is magnificent. One stalk will give you all the vitamin C you need for the entire day. Broccoli has more vitamin C than the same quantity of oranges. It also has vitamins A, B, calcium, iron and potassium. A full cup, which is high in fiber, contains only 40 calories.

GREEN BEANS PROVENCALE

1½ pounds fresh green beans,
    trimmed
4 ripe tomatoes
2 cloves garlic
Salt and freshly ground
    black pepper
1 tablespoon olive oil
3 tablespoons tomato paste
¼ teaspoon dried oregano
    (optional)
½ cup fresh parsley, chopped

1. Steam the beans for 6 minutes until crisp but not limp. Refresh the beans under cold running water.

2. Quarter the tomatoes and chop coarsely.

3. Chop and crush the garlic with a little salt to make a paste.

4. In a large skillet or saucepan, warm the olive oil over moderately high heat. Add the garlic paste, tomatoes, tomato paste and oregano, if used. Cook, stirring, for 3 to 4 minutes. Reduce the heat to moderately low and stir in the beans. Cook, tossing, until heated through.

5. Stir in the chopped parsley and serve hot.

Makes 8 servings

MONTEREY JACK CORN FRITTERS

1 cup yellow cornmeal
1 cup creamed corn
½ cup buttermilk
½ cup vegetable oil
1 cup Monterey Jack cheese,
    shredded
¾ teaspoon baking soda
Salt
2 teaspoons jalapeno pepper,
  finely chopped
1 egg
3 scallions, greens only, finely
    chopped
Unsalted butter, for the griddle

1. In a mixing bowl, blend together the cornmeal, creamed corn, buttermilk, vegetable oil, cheese, baking soda, salt, jalapeno pepper, egg and scallions.

2. Place a griddle over moderately high heat until hot. Lightly butter it and using about ¼ cup of the batter at a time, pour circles of batter onto the griddle. Cook until bubbles come to the surface. Flip the fritters and cook for a few minutes more.

Makes about 14 cakes

ABOUT BUTTERMILK

When special bacteria are mixed into fresh skim milk, part of the natural milk sugar converts to acid. The result is thick, smooth, tangy buttermilk. Buttermilk has less than one percent milk fat and only as many calories as the milk it was made from usually about 100 to 120 calories per cup. Like other milk products, buttermilk needs refrigeration. Keep it in a closed container. It should last 7 to 14 days.

SAUTEED EGGPLANT
WITH TOMATO FONDUE

1 large eggplant
Salt
1 tablespoon all-purpose flour
Freshly ground black pepper
About ½ cup vegetable oil
Tomato Fondue (see following
    recipe)
8 black olives

1. Preheat the oven to 400°F.

2. Trim both ends from the eggplant but do not peel. Cut, crosswise, into 8 thick slices. Sprinkle salt on both sides and place the slices flat on a board. Place a baking sheet on top of the slices and a weight on top of the sheet. Let stand about 20 minutes. (This removes excess liquid and any bitterness from the eggplant, and prevents it from absorbing too much oil during cooking.)

3. Dry the eggplant slices with paper towels. Lightly flour and pepper the slices.

4. Heat 2 tablespoons of the oil in a large skillet and fry the slices until lightly browned on both sides, adding more oil as needed.

5. Placed the browned eggplant slices in a shallow baking pan or dish. Place the pan on the top rack of the oven and bake for 7 minutes to finish cooking. Remove from the oven and keep warm.

6. Place 2 tablespoons of Tomato Fondue on each slice of eggplant and top with an olive.

Makes 4 servings

TOMATO FONDUE

3 to 4 large ripe tomatoes or use
   2 cups of skinless canned
   tomatoes and skip step
   number 1.
1 tablespoon unsalted butter
1 tablespoon vegetable oil
1 tablespoon onion, chopped
1 clove garlic, minced
Salt and freshly ground black
   pepper
1 tablespoon tomato paste

1. Dip the tomatoes in boiling water for 30 to 40 seconds; cool under cold running water. Slide the skins off.

2. Halve the tomatoes and squeeze out the seeds. Chop coarsely.

3. Place the butter and oil in a heavy skillet over moderate heat. Add the onion and garlic and saute for 1 minute, until softened but not browned.

4. Add the chopped tomatoes and salt and pepper to taste. Saute for 5 to 6 minutes, until the tomatoes are softened.

5. Stir in the tomato paste and cook 3 to 4 minutes more. Keep warm until ready to use.

BAKED SLICED POTATOES
WITH CHEESE & MUSTARD

4 tablespoons unsalted butter,
   at room temperature
½ cup prepared mustard
1 teaspoon salt
½ teaspoon freshly ground
   white pepper
2 pounds baking potatoes,
   peeled and thinly sliced
2 cups Swiss cheese, shredded
1¼ cups chicken stock

1. Preheat the oven to 425°F.

2. In a small bowl, blend the butter, mustard, salt and pepper together to form a smooth paste.

3. Butter a heatproof dish or pan that can be used as a serving dish. Arrange one-third of the potatoes in the dish. Dot the potatoes with one-third of the mustard mixture and one-third of the cheese.

4. Repeat this layering process twice again, until all of the potatoes and mustard mixture are used, ending with a layer of the remaining cheese.

5. Pour the chicken stock over the potatoes and place the baking dish on a baking sheet. Bake for 1 hour and 15 minutes, until bubbling and lightly browned. The baking sheet will catch any spillover from the baking dish.

Makes 6 servings

POTATOES GRATIN

1½ cups milk
1½ cups heavy cream
1 teaspoon salt
½ teaspoon freshly ground
    black pepper
2 cloves garlic, finely minced
1 tablespoon whole-grain
    mustard
2 pounds baking potatoes,
    scrubbed
¼ cup Parmesan cheese,
    freshly grated

1. Preheat the oven to 400°F. Lightly butter an 8-inch round heatproof baking dish or pan.

2. In a large saucepan, combine the milk, cream, salt, pepper, garlic and mustard.

3. Peel the potatoes and slice very thin. Put the slices directly into the milk/cream mixture to prevent them from turning brown.

4. Set the saucepan over moderate heat and stir until the liquid comes just to the boiling point. Watch carefully and stir to prevent scorching.

5. Pour the mixture into the prepared pan and sprinkle with the Parmesan cheese. Bake for 1 hour, or until a knife easily pierces the potatoes.

6. Remove to a rack to rest for about 15 minutes before serving.

Makes 4 to 6 servings

SALADS

SUNSET SALAD WITH LORENZO DRESSING

½ head green cabbage
½ head iceberg lettuce
5 thin slices cooked beef tongue
    or ham
2 chicken breasts, poached and
    skin and bone removed, or 1
    pound skinless, cooked turkey

1. Cut all of the above ingredients into thin match-size strips.

2. Combine all of the ingredients in a large bowl and toss with the Lorenzo dressing.

LORENZO DRESSING

½ cup chili sauce
½ cup watercress, finely chopped
½ cup French dressing

1. Combine the chili sauce and the watercress.

2. Add the French dressing and blend thoroughly.

Makes 4 servings

TOMATO, ONION AND GREEN BEAN SALAD

2 pounds fresh green beans,
  trimmed
3 large ripe tomatoes
2 tablespoons vegetable or olive
  oil
1 tablespoon red wine vinegar
1 small red onion, sliced

1. Steam the green beans for 7 minutes.

2. Slice the tomatoes and arrange them in an attractive pattern along the outside rim of a plate or platter.

3. Refresh the green beans under cold water. Pat dry and place them in the center of the tomatoes.

4. Pour the oil over the beans and tomatoes and sprinkle with vinegar.

5. Garnish with a few slices of red onion.

Makes 8 servings

ABOUT TOMATOES

Fresh tomatoes are high in vitamin C and fiber. They are a good source of vitamin A, potassium and contribute iron, the B vitamins, phosphorus and calcium. A medium-size tomato contains about 27 calories. Never store tomatoes in the refrigerator. Temperatures below 50°F. interfere with ripening. A refrigerated tomato will turn red but it will not become sweet and juicy. Store fresh tomatoes at room temperature, stem end up. The bumpy shoulders of the stem end are the most tender part of the tomato and will bruise simply by the weight of the fruit.

WALDORF SALAD

1½ cups red apple, cored,
  seeded and diced
1 tablespoon fresh lemon juice
1 cup celery, diced
½ cup mayonnaise
Lettuce leaves
Shelled walnuts
Jelly sandwiches

1. In a bowl, sprinkle the apple with lemon juice to prevent it from turning brown.

2. Add the celery and mayonnaise and mix well.

3. Arrange lettuce leaves on 2 serving plates. Spoon the apple and celery mixture on the lettuce leaves and garnish with walnuts. Serve with jelly sandwiches.

Makes 2 servings

STORING LEMONS
Place the lemons in a plastic bag and keep the bag in the refrigerator. That should keep them moist for about 2 weeks. A sliced lemon can hold for about 10 days if the exposed side is covered with plastic wrap and the piece is kept in a small tightly closed container.

CHICKEN, POTATO AND TOMATO SALAD WITH BASIL MAYONNAISE

One 3 to 4-pound chicken, freshly
  roasted and completely cooled
3 to 4 cups freshly cooked, new
  potatoes, cooled
¼ cup fresh basil leaves, tightly
  packed
1 tablespoon olive oil
⅔ cup mayonnaise, chilled
Salt and freshly ground black
  pepper
Fresh lemon juice
4 large ripe tomatoes

1. Remove the bones and skin and cut the chicken into 1-inch pieces. Cut the potatoes into 1-inch cubes and place both the chicken and potatoes in a large bowl.

2. In a blender or food processor puree the basil with the olive oil; there will be about 2 tablespoons of the puree. Mix the puree into the mayonnaise.

3. Add the mayonnaise mixture to the chicken and potatoes and toss lightly; season with salt, pepper and lemon juice to taste.

4. Slice the tomatoes and arrange on a serving dish. Spoon the salad into the center of the tomatoes and serve.

Makes 6 to 8 servings

MANDARIN CHICKEN SALAD

3 chicken breasts, poached, with
   bones and skin removed
2 cups fresh bean sprouts
2 tablespoons soy sauce
1 tablespoon white wine vinegar
1 tablespoon sesame oil
½ teaspoon chili oil
½ teaspoon sugar

1. Coarsely shred the cooked chicken breasts.

2. In a medium saucepan, boil the bean sprouts for 2 minutes. Refresh under cold water.

3. In a mixing bowl, combine the soy sauce, vinegar, sesame oil, chili oil and sugar.

4. Place the shredded chicken in a serving bowl, add the bean sprouts and the dressing. Stir together and serve.

Makes 4 to 6 servings

NOTE: This is a perfect warm weather picnic dish. There is no mayonnaise to worry about and the longer this dish marinates in its sauce, the better it tastes.

CURRIED CHICKEN SALAD

½ cup plain yogurt
½ cup mayonnaise
2 teaspoons curry powder
4 cups skinless boneless cooked
  chicken breast, diced
1 cup apple, chopped
1 cup walnuts, coarsely chopped
½ cup raisins

1. In a large bowl, blend together the yogurt and mayonnaise. Stir in the curry powder.

2. Add the chicken to the dressing and combine thoroughly. Stir in the apples, walnuts and raisins. Cover the bowl and refrigerate for 1 hour.

Makes 6 servings

ORANGE AND CUCUMBER SALAD

2 cucumbers, peeled and very
    thinly sliced
2 oranges, peeled and very thinly
    sliced
10 radishes, cleaned, very thinly
    sliced
Salt
1 tablespoon olive oil
Juice of 1 lemon

1. In a bowl, combine the cucumbers, oranges and radishes.

2. Add the salt, olive oil and lemon juice and toss. Serve at room temperature.

Makes 4 servings

ABOUT CUCUMBERS

Cucumbers are 96 percent water which makes them an ideal food for dieters. They are best stored, unwashed, in a plastic bag in the refrigerator. Put a few holes in the bag to allow a little air circulation. They should hold well for about 5 days.

Some old cookbooks suggest cut cucumbers be mixed with salt in order to draw out their water content. That may have been necessary at one time but todays varieties have a much different texture and the salting is not necessary.

SIENA SUMMER SALAD

1 cup water
3 cups stale Italian bread, broken
    into 1-inch cubes
1 cup lettuce, chopped
1 tomato, cut into ½-inch cubes
¼ cup fresh basil, minced, or
    1 teaspoon dried basil
¼ cup scallions, finely chopped
    (optional)
¼ cup gherkin pickles or
    cornichons, finely chopped
1 tablespoon anchovy fillets,
    chopped or anchovy paste
1 tablespoon capers
¼ cup olive oil
2 tablespoons red wine vinegar

1. In a bowl, soak the stale bread pieces in the water. Let the bread soak thoroughly for a moment, then drain and squeeze the bread until it is as dry as possible. Place the bread into a mixing bowl.

2. Add the lettuce, tomato, basil, scallions, gherkins, anchovies and capers and mix together. Add the olive oil and vinegar and mix again.

Makes 4 servings

NEW POTATO SALAD

3 pounds new potatoes, scrubbed
2 tablespoons salt
1 tablespoon caraway seeds
1 clove garlic
Salt and freshly ground black
    pepper
1 cup sour cream
¼ cup fresh dill, minced
Lettuce leaves, tomato wedges
    and a sprig of dill, for garnish

1. In a large saucepan, combine the potatoes, salt, caraway seeds, and garlic. Add water to cover and cook over moderately high heat for 20 minutes, or until the potatoes are tender. Drain and cool.

2. Quarter the potatoes and place in a mixing bowl. Add salt and pepper to taste and stir in the sour cream and dill.

3. Line a serving bowl with lettuce leaves, add the potato salad and garnish with tomato wedges and a sprig of dill.

Makes 6 servings

A LOW CALORIE SUBSTITUTE FOR SOUR CREAM

Combine 1 tablespoon fresh lemon juice, ⅓ cup buttermilk (made from skim or lowfat milk) and 1 cup of lowfat cottage cheese in a blender. Blend for 5 seconds. Use, volume for volume, as a substitute for sour cream.

CLASSIC AMERICAN COLESLAW

1½ cups mayonnaise
¼ cup prepared mustard
3 tablespoons white wine
  vinegar
1½ teaspoons dried tarragon
¼ teaspoon celery seed
Freshly ground pepper
10 cups green cabbage, shredded

1. In a large bowl, combine the mayonnaise, mustard, vinegar, tarragon and celery seed.

2. Add the cabbage to the dressing and mix until all the cabbage is evenly coated.

3. Cover and refrigerate briefly before serving.

Makes 10 servings

HOW TO BUY CABBAGE

Cabbage heads should feel solid and heavy in relation to their size. They should be closely trimmed, with stems cut close to the head and only 3 or 4 outer or wrapper leaves. The cabbage should show no discolored veins and the outer leaves should have a fresh appearance, with no sign of puffiness or wormholes. Undamaged, unwashed heads can be stored in a plastic bag in the refrigerator for a week to 10 days.

Raw cabbage is rich in vitamin C and has a fair amount of vitamin B. Cabbage also has significant amounts of calcium, phosphorus and potassium. One cup of finely shredded cabbage contains 24 calories.

SAUCES & DRESSINGS

THOUSAND ISLAND DRESSING

1 cup mayonnaise
½ cup chili sauce
1 hard-cooked egg, chopped
1 tablespoon dill pickle, chopped
1½ teaspoons fresh parsley,
   minced
1 teaspoon Worcestershire sauce

1. In a mixing bowl, combine the mayonnaise and chili sauce.

2. Stir in the hard-cooked egg, pickles, parsley and Worcestershire sauce.

Makes about 1½ cups

NOTE: For many years Thousand Island has been the most popular salad dressing in the United States, valuable information when you're making a salad dressing for new guests.

CREOLE MAYONNAISE

¼ cup celery, chopped
2 tablespoons fresh parsley,
  chopped
2 tablespoons onion, chopped
1 teaspoon Worcestershire sauce
2 tablespoons red wine vinegar
¼ cup Creole mustard or other
  hot and spicy mustard
2 tablespoons prepared white
  horseradish
2 tablespoons paprika
1 teaspoon salt
½ teaspoon freshly ground black
  pepper
2 cups mayonnaise

1. In a large bowl, combine all of the ingredients and mix thoroughly.

2. Cover and refrigerate.

Makes 1 quart

NOTE: Creole is a word used to describe the descendants of the original settlers of New Orleans. Their special style of cooking has been the basis for much of the fame that surrounds Southern Louisiana cooking.

This Creole mayonnaise is ideal as a dip for fresh vegetables. Mixed with shredded cabbage it makes a very tasty cole slaw. Put a light coating over fish or poultry before broiling. Use it as a dipping sauce for seafood, poultry or vegetables.

BLUE CHEESE DRESSING

½ cup crumbled blue cheese
1 teaspoon dry mustard
¼ cup red wine vinegar
Freshly ground black pepper
2 cups mayonnaise or plain
   lowfat yogurt

1. In a bowl, mix together the blue cheese, mustard, vinegar and pepper to taste until completely blended.

2. Add the mayonnaise or yogurt and mix well. Cover and refrigerate for up to 10 days.

Makes 2 cups

STORING BLUE CHEESE
A small piece (4 ounces) of blue cheese will hold properly in the refrigerator for about 4 weeks. The larger the block of blue cheese the better it will store. Wrap the cheese in a piece of moist cheesecloth. Wrap the cheesecloth with plastic wrap and place it into a tightly closed container. Each week, open the container, moisten the cheesecloth, rewrap and refrigerate the container. The cheese will keep for 2 months or longer. Cut off only what you are going to use and keep the cheese under almost constant refrigeration.

REMOULADE SAUCE

6 tablespoons Creole or other hot
   and spicy mustard
1 teaspoon prepared white
   horseradish
3 tablespoons garlic, chopped
⅓ cup celery, chopped
⅓ cup dill pickles, chopped
3 tablespoons fresh parsley,
   chopped
⅓ cup scallions, chopped
⅔ cup vegetable oil
⅓ cup white wine vinegar
Dash of Worcestershire sauce
5 drops Tabasco sauce

1. In a mixing bowl, combine the mustard, horseradish, garlic, celery, pickles, parsley and scallions. Blend together.

2. Whisk in the vegetable oil, vinegar, Worcestershire sauce and Tabasco sauce.

Makes 1½ cups

NOTE: This sauce makes an excellent dip for raw vegetables or a dressing for salads. It is also a fine sauce to pour over cooked shellfish.

CREAMY RASPBERRY DRESSING

1 egg
2 cups vegetable oil
½ cup red wine vinegar
One 10-ounce package frozen
    raspberries, thawed

1. Whip the egg until it starts to foam. Begin adding the oil very slowly. When it starts to thicken, add the vinegar until it is thoroughly combined.

2. In a food processor, puree the raspberries.

3. Add the oil mixture and process until combined. If the raspberries are tart, a little sugar may be added.

Makes 1 quart

ABOUT FROZEN FRUITS
Frozen fruits have a tendency to thaw very rapidly. It is a good idea to buy frozen foods at the end of your shopping. Keep them on top of your groceries and get them into your freezer as quickly as possible. In a freezer that is kept at 0°F. or below, frozen fruit will keep for 9 months to a year.

CREAMY TARRAGON DRESSING

1 egg
1 tablespoon Dijon-style mustard
2 cups vegetable oil
¼ cup red wine vinegar
1 tablespoon dried tarragon
Salt and freshly ground black
   pepper

1. In a food processor or blender or in a bowl with a whisk, beat together the egg and mustard until foamy. Very slowly add the oil until thickened. Add the vinegar and beat until thoroughly combined.

2. Stir in the tarragon and salt and pepper to taste.

Makes 2 cups

ABOUT PEPPER
A peppercorn (whole) will keep its potency for over 5 years. At the moment you break the kernel the flavor is at its peak. Black pepper is slightly more pungent than white pepper. White pepper is sometimes preferred on light colored sauces and foods.

WALNUT DRESSING

2 tablespoons fresh lemon juice
⅓ cup fresh orange juice
2 teaspoons prepared mustard
1 clove garlic, finely chopped
⅓ cup vegetable oil
Pinch of salt
⅓ cup walnuts, chopped

1. In a bowl, mix together the lemon and orange juices, mustard and garlic.

2. Slowly whisk in the vegetable oil and continue whisking until well mixed.

3. Stir in the salt and walnuts.

Makes 1 cup

HOW TO STORE GARLIC

Do not store garlic in the refrigerator or in a plastic bag. The moisture will shorten its life. I like to store garlic by taking the skin off the cloves and popping them into a jar of vegetable oil. Then cover with a tight lid. The oil acts as a natural preservative. Held in the refrigerator, the garlic will last for months. Also, the oil will pick up the flavor of the garlic and you can use the oil to flavor your cooking and dressings.

The easiest way to get the skin off the clove is to trim the tips off and gently hit the clove with the side of a knife. That will loosen the skin and it should come away easily.

DESSERTS

CHIMNEY SWEEP

2 scoops vanilla ice cream
1 heaping tablespoon finely
    ground dark roast coffee or
    espresso beans
1 tablespoon Scotch whiskey, or
    fruit juice

1. Mound the ice cream into a glass or bowl.
2. Sprinkle the ground coffee over the ice cream.
3. Pour the Scotch on top and serve.

Makes 1 serving

NOTE: You can make powdered espresso by pulverizing coffee
beans in a coffee mill or blender. Or you can use instant
espresso coffee powder.

CHOCOLATE LOAF

3 cups heavy cream
1¼ pounds semisweet chocolate,
    grated
4 egg yolks
¼ pound unsalted butter, at room
    temperature
½ cup almonds, blanched and
    slivered
Strawberries or raspberries,
    for serving
Heavy cream, whipped and
    sweetened, for serving

1. Lightly butter a 9 x 5 x 3-inch loaf pan. Line the inside with waxed paper, cut to fit.

2. In a small saucepan, scald the heavy cream until hot, but not boiling. Remove from the heat. Add the chocolate and whisk until smooth and melted. One at a time, add the egg yolks, whisking after each addition. Cover and refrigerate to cool completely.

3. When cooled, whisk in the butter. Add the almonds and pour the mixture into the prepared loaf pan. Refrigerate overnight.

4. To serve, dip the loaf pan into warm water for 30 seconds, to loosen the loaf from the pan. Remove the pan from the water and invert it onto a serving plate to free the loaf. Remove the waxed paper.

5. Serve plain or slice and decorate with strawberries or raspberries and sweetened whipped cream.

Makes 8 servings

CHOCOLATE TRUFFLES

⅓ cup heavy cream
2 tablespoons unsalted butter
6 ounces semisweet chocolate,
    grated, coarsely chopped or
    broken into small pieces
Unsweetened cocoa powder
Chopped nuts
Confectioners' sugar

1. In a small saucepan over moderate heat, or in the top of a double boiler over simmering water, heat the cream and butter, stirring until the butter is melted and the cream just starts to come to a boil; do not let the cream boil.

2. Remove from the heat, and add the chocolate and stir until completely melted.

3. Cover and chill in the refrigerator for at least 2 hours, stirring occasionally, until the mixture is firm.

4. Using a pastry bag or a spoon, make small balls of the chocolate mixture. Roll each truffle in cocoa powder, chopped nuts, confectioners' sugar or leave as is. Refrigerate in an airtight container until needed. If you can resist, let come to room temperature before serving.

Makes about 24 truffles

COFFEE MOUSSE

1 cup heavy cream
2 tablespoons plus 2 teaspoons
   sugar
1½ teaspoons powdered instant
   coffee
2 ounces semisweet chocolate,
   melted
1 egg white

1. With an electric mixer, beat the cream, 2 tablespoons of the sugar and the instant coffee until stiff peaks form and cream is very thick. Stir in the chocolate.

2. In another bowl, beat the egg white with the remaining 2 teaspoons sugar until stiff.

3. Gently fold the egg white mixture into the coffee mixture and combine. Spoon the mixture into a bowl or stemmed glasses. Chill for 2 hours.

Makes 4 servings

TIPS ON WHIPPING CREAM
The secret to getting heavy cream to whip properly is to use very fresh cream and keep it in the refrigerator for at least 2 hours before you whip it. Shake the carton before whipping and chill the bowl and beater in the freezer for 30 minutes before you start.

CHOCOLATE CHIP MOUSSE

4 egg whites
1 cup sugar
8 ounces milk chocolate, melted
2 cups heavy cream
3 ounces semisweet chocolate,
    chopped into small bits
Heavy cream, whipped and
    sweetened, for serving

1. Combine the egg whites and the sugar in the top of a double boiler or in a large metal bowl set over simmering water. Beat constantly until the sugar dissolves and the mixture is heated through, about 3 minutes. The mixture should be hot to the touch.

2. Remove from the heat and beat for 3 to 5 minutes or until the mixture cools to 115°F. or less.

3. Pour the cooled chocolate into the egg white mixture and stir together.

4. Whip the heavy cream until very thick and stiff.

5. Gently fold the whipped cream into the chocolate mixture with a spatula.

6. Fold in the chocolate bits.

7. Pour the mixture into a serving bowl or individual glasses and refrigerate for at least 1 hour. Just before serving, top with whipped cream.

Makes 4 servings

HOT CHOCOLATE SOUFFLE

1½ tablespoons powdered instant
    espresso coffee, or 2
    tablespoons instant coffee
    powder
1½ tablespoons boiling water
6 ounces unsweetened chocolate,
    grated or broken into small
    pieces
⅓ cup cornstarch
1½ cups milk
1½ cups plus 2 tablespoons sugar
7 eggs, separated
Pinch of salt
¼ teaspoon cream of tartar
Heavy cream, whipped and
    sweetened or vanilla ice
    cream, for serving

1. Preheat the oven to 350°F.

2. Lightly butter and sugar an 8-inch souffle mold, tapping on all sides to coat evenly with sugar. Chill until needed.

3. In the top of a double boiler set over simmering water, dissolve the instant coffee in the boiling water. Add the chocolate and stir until just melted. Set aside to cool.

4. In a saucepan, combine the cornstarch and ¼ cup of the milk. Whisk until smooth, then whisk in the remaining 1¼ cups milk and 1½ cups of the sugar. Set over moderate heat and bring to a boil, whisking constantly to prevent scorching. Boil for 30 seconds.

5. Transfer the mixture to a large bowl, beat in the egg yolks, one at a time, incorporating thoroughly after each addition. Mix in the melted chocolate mixture.

6. In another bowl, beat the egg whites with an electric mixer at high speed until they start to foam. Add the salt and cream of tartar. Continue beating at high speed until the whites are stiff but not dry. Add the remaining 2 tablespoons sugar and beat just to incorporate.

7. Fold the egg whites into the chocolate mixture with a rubber spatula. Pour the batter into the prepared soüffle mold and bake for 40 minutes, without opening the oven during the baking time. Serve immediately with sweetened whipped cream or vanilla ice cream.

Makes 6 servings

PREPARING A SOUFFLE MOLD
When a souffle batter is heated, it starts to rise up along the walls of the souffle mold. If the walls are smooth, the batter will slip back a little as it goes up. If you butter the inside of the mold and then give it a little coating of sugar or bread crumbs (depending on the souffle) and refrigerate the mold for 30 minutes, the texture of the inside surface will then be like sandpaper. The rough texture gives the batter a ladder to climb up. The souffle will rise with greater ease.

STRAWBERRY SOUFFLE

1½ cups fresh or frozen
   strawberries, chopped
7 tablespoons sugar
1 tablespoon Grand Marnier or
   other orange flavored liqueur
3 tablespoons unsalted butter
2 tablespoons all-purpose flour
½ cup milk
6 eggs, separated

1. In a bowl, combine the strawberries, 2 tablespoons of sugar and the Grand Marnier. Let stand about 15 minutes.

2. Preheat the oven to 400°F. Lightly butter a 9-inch souffle mold or deep baking dish. Sprinkle it with sugar, tilting the dish to coat thoroughly.

3. Melt the butter in a saucepan over moderate heat and stir in the flour. Cook, stirring constantly for 2 to 3 minutes. Gradually add the milk and stir until the mixture is thickened and smooth.

4. Remove from the heat. One at a time, beat in the egg yolks and 3 tablespoons of the sugar. Stir in the strawberry mixture. Set aside.

5. About 30 minutes before serving, beat the egg whites until stiff. Add the remaining 2 tablespoons sugar and beat for 1 to 2 minutes until combined. Gently fold the egg whites into the strawberry mixture.

6. Pour the mixture into the prepared mold and bake for 20 to 25 minutes. Serve immediately.

Makes 6 servings

APPLE AND RAISIN CRUNCH

½ cup raisins
Boiling water
6 tart apples (such as Granny
    Smiths), cored, peeled and
    sliced
Grated zest and juice of 1 lemon
¼ to ½ cup sugar, depending on
    the sweetness of the apples
1 teaspoon ground cinnamon
½ teaspoon ground nutmeg
4 cups packed fresh, unflavored
    white bread crumbs (about
    ¾ loaf with crusts removed
    and run through a food
    processor or blender)
¼ pound unsalted butter, melted
Ice cream, for serving

1. Preheat the oven to 400°F. Lightly butter a 10-inch pie pan.

2. In a small bowl, cover the raisins with boiling water. Set aside to soften.

3. As you slice the apples, toss with lemon juice to prevent browning. Add the lemon zest, sugar, cinnamon and nutmeg and mix well. Set aside.

4. In a bowl, combine the bread crumbs and butter. Mix thoroughly.

5. Drain the raisins.

6. Spread about one third of the bread crumbs in the bottom of the prepared pan. Top with half of the apple slices, and half of the raisins. Repeat the process, ending with bread crumbs. Cover with a sheet of buttered aluminum foil.

7. Bake for 25 minutes. Remove the foil and bake for about 10 minutes until golden.

8. Serve warm, as is, or with ice cream.

Makes 6 servings

ABOUT RAISINS

Raisins are dried grapes. The moisture in the fruit has been reduced to a point that prevents the development of many of the enzymes that cause spoilage. To store raisins properly they should be removed from the packaging they were purchased in and placed into a plastic, steel, glass or ceramic container with a tight fitting lid. The container should be stored in the refrigerator. If the raisins become hard during storage they can be soaked until tender in water or fruit juice.

POACHED PINEAPPLE IN MAPLE SYRUP

1 large pineapple
2 cups maple syrup
2 cups plain yogurt

1. Peel and core the pineapple. Slice the pineapple crosswise into ½-inch slices.

2. In a heavy saucepan, bring the maple syrup to a boil. Add the sliced pineapple and remove the pan from the heat. Allow the pineapple and maple syrup to sit in the saucepan until the syrup is cool.

3. Serve the pineapple at room temperature, drizzled with a few tablespoons of maple syrup. Serve the yogurt on the side as a topping.

Makes 6 servings

STORING PINEAPPLES

The best way to store a whole ripe pineapple is in a closed plastic bag in the refrigerator. The pineapple will keep for about 4 days. If you need to hold the pineapple for a longer period of time, cut off the fruit's outer skin. Remove the core and cut the meat into 1-inch chunks. Store the pineapple pieces and their juices in a tightly closed container in the refrigerator. That process will hold the pineapple for about one week.

BANANAS FOSTER

4 tablespoons unsalted butter
1 cup brown sugar
Pinch of ground cinnamon
4 bananas, peeled and halved
    lengthwise
¼ cup rum (an optional
    ingredient, you may skip the
    rum and go directly to the ice
    cream)
Vanilla ice cream, for serving

1. In a saute pan, combine the butter, brown sugar and cinnamon over moderate heat. Stir and cook for about 3 minutes, until the sugar dissolves.

2. Add the bananas to the butter and sugar mixture and cook for 30 seconds. Stir in the rum. Cook for 1 minute. Very carefully, ignite the sauce, shaking the pan until the flames subside. Serve the bananas over vanilla ice cream and spoon the sauce over the top.

Makes 4 servings

BROWN SUGAR TIPS

The best way to store leftover brown sugar is in an airtight container. Add a slice of apple or a lettuce leaf to it before closing it up. The moisture in the apple or lettuce will help keep the moist texture that you find in fresh brown sugar. You can also use this technique to soften brown sugar that has hardened. If you need to soften hard sugar immediately, put it into a blender or food processor.

ZABAGLIONE WITH FRESH STRAWBERRIES

1 pint fresh strawberries, washed
   and stemmed
8 egg yolks
½ cup sugar
½ to ⅔ cup Marsala or sweet
   sherry wine (to taste)

1. Divide the strawberries among six stemmed glasses.

2. Combine the egg yolks, sugar and Marsala in the top of a large double boiler and place over simmering water. Cook, beating the mixture rapidly with a wire whisk until it becomes a thick creamy custard.

3. Immediately pour the custard over the strawberries and serve at once.

Makes 6 servings

NOTE: If strawberries are not available, substitute sliced fresh, frozen or canned peaches, pitted fresh or canned apricot halves or sliced bananas. Be sure to fully drain frozen or canned fruit before serving.

CAKES, PIES, TARTS & COOKIES

HARRY'S CHEESECAKE

3 pounds (six 8-ounce packages)
   cream cheese, at room
   temperature
2¼ cups sugar
6 eggs
3 tablespoons cornstarch
1½ cups heavy cream
4 tablespoons unsalted butter
1 tablespoon vanilla extract
Juice of 1 lemon

1. Preheat the oven to 350°F. Butter a 12 x 18-inch oblong baking pan or two 10-inch springform pans.

2. In the bowl of an electric mixer combine the cream cheese, sugar, eggs, cornstarch, heavy cream, butter, vanilla and lemon juice. Beat until fluffy and well mixed.

3. Pour the mixture into the prepared pan and set the pan into a larger pan. Add enough water to the outside pan to reach halfway up the outside of the cheesecake pan.

4. Bake for 1 hour. To prevent cracking, do not open the oven during baking.

5. Remove the cheesecake pan to a rack and allow the cake to cool completely before serving.

Makes about 20 servings

FLOURLESS CHOCOLATE CAKE

10 ounces semisweet chocolate
7 tablespoons unsalted butter
7 eggs, separated
⅓ cup sugar

1. Preheat the oven to 275°F. Butter and flour a 10-inch springform pan or deep cake pan.

2. In the top of a double boiler, over simmering water, melt the chocolate and butter until smooth. Remove from the heat.

3. In a mixing bowl, beat the egg whites until slightly stiff. Add the sugar and beat for 30 seconds, until stiff.

4. Whisk the egg yolks into the slightly cooled chocolate mixture.

5. Gently fold the chocolate mixture into the beaten egg whites mixing only until no white streaks remain.

6. Pour the cake batter into the pan and bake for 30 to 40 minutes.

7. If you are using a springform pan, release the sides of the pan and let cool on a wire rack. If not, place a sheet of parchment paper on a baking sheet and place the baking sheet, parchment paper facing down, over the cake. Invert the pan to release the cake and set the cake pan aside. Set a wire rack over the cake and invert again so that the top side is up. Allow to cool for 1 hour.

Makes 8 servings

GLAZED APPLESAUCE CAKE

¼ pound unsalted butter
1¼ cups sugar
1 egg
2 cups sweetened or
    unsweetened applesauce
2¼ cups all-purpose flour
1 teaspoon ground cinnamon
½ teaspoon ground nutmeg
⅛ teaspoon ground cloves
¼ teaspoon salt
2 teaspoons baking soda
½ cup pecan halves
1 apple, peeled, cored and finely
    diced
1 apple, peeled, cored and thinly
    sliced
1 cup apricot jam
¼ cup honey
1 tablespoon water

1. Preheat the oven to 350°F. Butter and flour a 9-inch springform pan.

2. In a mixing bowl, cream the butter and gradually add the sugar. Beat until light and fluffy. Beat in the egg and blend in the applesauce.

3. Sift together the dry ingredients. Fold the mixture into the cake batter. Add the pecans and diced apple.

4. Pour the mixture into the prepared pan and arrange the apple slices decoratively on top.

5. Bake for 1¼ hours. Remove to a rack and allow to cool. Release the sides of the pan.

6. Prepare the glaze: In a small saucepan, combine the apricot jam, honey and water over low heat. Stir until melted and smooth. Brush the top of the cooled cake with the apricot-honey glaze.

Makes 8 servings

CARROT CAKE WITH CREAM CHEESE ICING

2 cups sugar
1½ cups vegetable oil
4 eggs, lightly beaten
2 cups all-purpose flour
1 teaspoon salt
2 teaspoons baking soda
2 teaspoons ground cinnamon
½ teaspoon ground nutmeg
½ teaspoon ground allspice
3 cups carrots, finely shredded
   (6 to 8 carrots)
½ cup walnuts, chopped

Cream cheese icing:
¼ pound unsalted butter, at room
   temperature
One 8-ounce package cream
   cheese, at room temperature
2 cups confectioners' sugar
2 teaspoons vanilla extract

1. Preheat the oven to 325°F. Butter a 13 x 9 x 2-inch baking pan.

2. In an electric mixer or by hand, thoroughly mix together the sugar, oil and eggs.

3. Sift together the flour, salt, baking soda and spices. Gradually add the flour mixture to the egg mixture blending well before adding more.

4. Fold in the carrots and walnuts. Pour the batter into the prepared pan and bake for 1 hour to 1 hour and 10 minutes, until a toothpick inserted into the center comes out clean. Remove to a rack to cool to room temperature.

5. Make the icing: Cream the butter until light and fluffy.

6. Mash the cream cheese with a fork and work it into the butter. Add the confectioners' sugar and vanilla and beat vigorously, until blended.

7. When the cake is cool, spread with the cream cheese icing.

Makes 12 servings

SWEET SPICES

For hundreds of years sugar was hard to get and it was expensive. Cooks developed ways of increasing the sweetening effect of sugar by using what are called "sweet spices." These seasonings are not necessarily sweet by themselves but seem to enhance the sweet flavor of other ingredients. The sweet spices include cinnamon, cloves, nutmeg, allspice and ginger.

NEW YORK CHOCOLATE CHEESECAKE

6 ounces bittersweet chocolate,
  grated or broken into pieces
2 pounds (four 8-ounce packages)
  cream cheese, at room
  temperature
1¾ cups sugar
4 eggs
1 teaspoon vanilla extract

1. Preheat the oven to 350°F. Lightly butter a 9-inch springform pan. Line the bottom with a circle of waxed paper and butter the paper.

2. Melt the chocolate in the top of a double boiler, set over hot water. Set aside.

3. In a large bowl, beat the cream cheese with an electric mixer at high speed until fluffy. Gradually add the sugar, and beat until the mixture is smooth and the sugar is dissolved. Add the eggs, one at a time, mixing well after each addition and scrape the batter down the sides of the bowl with a rubber spatula. Stir in the vanilla.

4. In a bowl, combine one quarter of the cream cheese mixture with the melted chocolate.

5. Pour the remaining cream cheese mixture into the prepared mold.

6. Pour the chocolate-cream cheese mixture into the center of the mold. With a knife, draw lines through the batter to mix in the chocolate and give the cake a marbleized look.

7. Set the pan into a larger pan. Add enough water to the outer pan to reach halfway up the sides of the springform pan.

8. Bake for 1¼ to 1½ hours, until a toothpick inserted in the center comes out clean.

9. Invert the cake onto a dish, then invert again onto a serving plate. Cover with plastic wrap to prevent the cake from absorbing odors. Set it to cool in the refrigerator for at least 2 hours.

Makes 8 servings

ABOUT COOKING WITH CHOCOLATE

Chocolate and cocoa powder are sensitive to heat, moisture and odors. They should be stored in a closed container, in a dry place at a moderately cool temperature, between 55° and 70°F.

The best way to melt chocolate is in the top of a double boiler. Make sure that the water is not boiling, because chocolate should be melted by the water's heat and not by steam. Steam is too hot and could burn the chocolate.

Water does not mix well with melting chocolate. Any pots and utensils used in working with chocolate should be completely dry. Even a small amount of water can cause melted chocolate to thicken and tighten. If by accident you end up with thickened chocolate you can correct the problem by adding a small amount of vegetable shortening to the chocolate and whisking everything back to a smooth consistency.

LEMON TART

Prebaked 9-inch tart shell
5 eggs
1 cup superfine sugar
7 tablespoons unsalted butter
   clarified and cooled
½ cup fresh lemon juice
Zest of 1 orange, finely grated
Confectioners' sugar (optional),
   for dusting the tart

1. Preheat the oven to 325°F. Place the tart pan on a baking sheet.

2. With an electric mixer, beat together the eggs and sugar. Gradually add the clarified butter and blend well. Stir in the lemon juice and orange zest.

3. Place the baking sheet and tart shell into the oven. Pour the egg and lemon mixture into the crust.

4. Bake for 25 minutes, or until the liquid has set.

5. Remove to a rack to cool to room temperature. Dust lightly with confectioners' sugar before serving.

Makes 8 servings

NOTE: In step 3, you are asked to pour the batter into the shell after the tart pan has been placed in the oven. The batter-filled crust spills easily; putting it in the oven first saves a move.

HOW TO MAKE CLARIFIED BUTTER
Clarified butter is regular butter from which certain substances have been removed. It can be heated to a much higher temperature than whole butter, without burning. It also stores better. Cut regular unsalted butter into small pieces. Put them into a heatproof measuring cup. Put the cup into an oven that's set to its lowest temperature. When the butter is melted, there will be three distinct layers in the cup. Skim off and discard the top foamy layer. Carefully pour off the middle layer which is the clarified butter. Leave the bottom layer behind and discard.

GREAT AMERICAN BROWNIES

4 ounces unsweetened chocolate
¼ pound unsalted butter, at room
    temperature
4 eggs
2 cups sugar
1 teaspoon vanilla extract
1 cup all-purpose flour
½ teaspoon salt
1½ cups walnuts, chopped

1. Preheat the oven to 325°F. Lightly butter a 9-inch square baking pan.

2. In the top of a double boiler set over simmering water, melt the chocolate and butter. Set aside to cool slightly.

3. With an electric mixer at high speed, beat the eggs and gradually add the sugar. Beat until the mixture is pale yellow and the sugar is dissolved, about 5 minutes.

4. Add the melted chocolate and the vanilla. Stir in the flour, salt and nuts.

5. Pour the batter into the prepared pan and bake for 40 to 45 minutes, or until a toothpick inserted in the center comes out clean.

6. Remove to a rack to cool, before cutting the brownies into squares.

Makes 16 brownies

OLD-FASHIONED STRAWBERRY SHORTCAKES

Shortcake:
4 cups all-purpose flour
¼ cup plus 2 tablespoons sugar
1 tablespoon plus 2 teaspoons
    baking powder
1 teaspoon salt
¼ pound plus 4 tablespoons
    unsalted butter, chilled and cut
    into bits
1½ cups heavy cream
2 tablespoons unsalted butter,
    melted and cooled

Topping:
2 pints fresh ripe strawberries,
    washed and stemmed
2 tablespoons sugar, or to taste
Heavy cream, whipped and
    sweetened, for serving

1. Preheat the oven to 425°F. Lightly butter a large baking sheet.

2. In a large bowl mix together the flour, sugar, baking powder and salt. Add the butter, and with a pastry blender or fingertips, rub the butter into the dry ingredients until the mixture resembles coarse meal.

3. Add the cream and mix thoroughly until a soft dough forms.

4. Gather the dough into a compact disc and place on a lightly floured board or work surface. Knead the dough for about 1 minute, folding it end to end and pressing down and pushing forward several times with the heel of your hand.

5. Roll out the dough into a ½-inch-thick circle. With a 3-inch cookie cutter, cut out 9 rounds. With a 2½-inch cookie cutter, cut the remaining dough into 9 rounds. (If there isn't enough dough, gather the scraps, knead briefly and roll out again.) Arrange the 3-inch rounds on the prepared baking sheet. Brush each with melted butter and top with a smaller round.

6. Bake in the center of the oven for 15 minutes, until firm to the touch and golden brown. Remove to a rack to cool.

7. Coarsely chop half the strawberries, reserving the most attractive ones for the top.

8. Pull the smaller tops away from the bottoms of the shortcakes. Spread a layer of chopped strawberries on the bottom halves, sprinkle each with sugar and gently cover with the top halves. Garnish with whole strawberries and whipped cream.

Makes 8 servings

NOTE: Traditionally, Old-Fashioned Strawberry Shortcake was served with heavy unwhipped cream simply poured over it. Nowadays, it's usually topped with whipped cream.

PECAN PIE

Dough:
1 cup all-purpose flour, sifted
  twice
½ teaspoon salt
⅓ cup vegetable shortening
3 tablespoons ice water

Filling:
6 eggs
¾ cup dark brown sugar, firmly
  packed
¾ cup white sugar
1½ cups dark corn syrup
1½ tablespoons all-purpose flour
4 tablespoons unsalted butter,
  melted
1 tablespoon vanilla extract
1½ cups pecans, cut into pieces
  (6 ounces)
Heavy cream, whipped and
  sweetened or vanilla ice
  cream, for serving

1. Prepare the dough: In a large bowl, sift together the flour and salt. Cut in the vegetable shortening until the mixture resembles coarse meal. Sprinkle on the ice water and toss with 2 forks until the dough pulls together into a ball. Do not handle.

2. Shape the dough into a fat disc. Wrap in plastic and refrigerate for at least 1 hour.

3. Preheat the oven to 350°F.

4. On a well floured surface, roll out the dough ⅛-inch thick. Press the dough into a 10-inch pie pan and flute the edges. Set the pie pan on a baking sheet.

5. Prepare the filling: In a bowl, beat the eggs and stir in the sugars, corn syrup, flour, butter and vanilla. Mix until well blended. Add the pecans and mix again.

6. Pour the filling into the prepared shell (the pecans will rise to the top) and bake for 40 minutes, or until the back of spoon pressed in the center of the filling feels solid and no liquid comes to the surface.

7. Remove to a rack to cool. Serve with sweetened whipped cream or vanilla ice cream.

Makes 8 servings

ABOUT CORN SYRUP

Corn syrup is a liquid sugar. It is used in candy making and baking because it does not form cyrstals when cooked. A bottle of corn syrup that has been opened will keep for 4 months. It is valuable to date the bottle with a marker when you open it.

Before you measure liquid sugars (like corn syrup or honey) coat the measuring spoon or cup with a little vegetable oil or butter. The grease will keep the liquid sugar from sticking to the surface of the measuring tool.

CHOCOLATE SILK PIE

One 8½-ounce box chocolate
   wafers
6 tablespoons unsalted butter,
   melted
7 ounces bittersweet chocolate,
   grated or finely chopped
½ pound unsalted butter
1½ cups sugar
2 teaspoons vanilla extract
4 eggs
Heavy cream, whipped and
   sweetened, for serving

1. Prepare the crust: Put the chocolate wafers in a food processor or blender and process until finely crushed. Mix the crumbs with the melted butter. Evenly press the mixture into the bottom and sides of an 8-inch pie pan.

2. Prepare the filling: In the top of a double boiler set over simmering water, melt the chocolate. Set aside to cool slightly.

3. In a large bowl, beat the remaining butter and sugar together with an electric mixer at high speed until the mixture is light and fluffy, about 10 minutes.

4. Blend in the cooled chocolate and the vanilla. One at a time, add the eggs, beating thoroughly after each addition.

5. Pour the filling into the pie crust and refrigerate for at least 3 hours. Serve with sweetened whipped cream.

Makes 8 servings

APPLE TARTS WITH ALMONDS

¾ cup all-purpose flour
7 tablespoons unsalted butter,
   at room temperature
2 tablespoons ice water
4 medium Golden Delicious
   apples
1 cup sliced almonds
3 tablespoons granulated sugar
Confectioners' sugar

1. Preheat the oven to 450°F. Line 2 baking sheets with parchment paper.

2. In a large mixing bowl, pinch together the flour and 4 tablespoons of the butter with your fingers. After a few moments, add the ice water and shape the dough into a disc. Wrap in plastic and refrigerate for at least 30 minutes.

3. Divide the dough into 4 pieces. Roll out each piece into a 5-inch circle. Place the circles on the prepared sheets.

4. Peel, core and thinly slice the apples.

5. Arrange the apple slices in an overlapping circular pattern on each disc of dough. Melt the remaining 3 tablespoons of butter and brush onto the apples. Sprinkle with the almonds and sugar and bake for 12 to 15 minutes.

6. Just before serving, sprinkle the tarts with confectioners' sugar.

Makes 4 tarts

OATMEAL RAISIN COOKIES

¼ pound unsalted butter, at room
  temperature
¾ cup white sugar
¾ cup brown sugar
2 eggs
1 teaspoon vanilla extract
1¾ cups all-purpose flour
1 teaspoon ground cinnamon
1 teaspoon baking soda
½ teaspoon salt
2 cups rolled oats (not the "quick-
  cooking" type)
1 cup raisins

1. Preheat the oven to 375°F. Lightly butter a baking sheet.

2. In a bowl with an electric mixer at high speed, cream the butter and white sugar until light and fluffy, 3 to 5 minutes. Gradually add the brown sugar. One at a time, add the eggs, and the vanilla; blend well.

3. Sift together the flour, cinnamon, baking soda and salt. A small amount at a time, add to the butter mixture, mixing well after each addition. Fold in the oats and raisins.

4. Drop the cookies by heaping teaspoonfuls onto the baking sheet, about 2 inches apart. Bake for 10 to 12 minutes.

Makes about 60 cookies.

TRIPLE CHOCOLATE CHUNK NUT COOKIES

6 ounces semisweet chocolate
2 ounces bittersweet chocolate
6 tablespoons unsalted butter
2 eggs
1 tablespoon powdered instant
   espresso coffee
2 teaspoons vanilla extract
¾ cup white sugar
⅓ cup all-purpose flour
1 teaspoon baking powder
¼ teaspoon salt
1 cup walnut pieces
1 cup pecan pieces
6 ounces milk chocolate, cut into
   small bits

1. Preheat the oven to 325°F. Lightly butter a baking sheet and line with waxed or parchment paper.

2. In the top of a double boiler combine the semisweet chocolate, the bittersweet chocolate and the butter over simmering water. Melt, stirring from time to time, until smooth. Set aside to cool.

3. In a bowl with an electric mixer on low speed, mix the eggs, espresso and vanilla. At high speed, gradually add the sugar and beat until the mixture is thick and light.

4. In another bowl, mix the flour, baking powder and salt together. Set aside.

5. Add the melted chocolate mixture to the egg mixture. Beat on low speed until well blended. Gradually add the flour mixture and beat on low speed. Stir in the nuts and milk chocolate bits and mix well.

6. Drop the cookies by heaping tablespoonfuls, onto the prepared baking sheet, 2 inches apart. Bake for 15 to 20 minutes.

Makes about 15 cookies

PEANUT BUTTER PEANUT COOKIES

½ pound unsalted butter, at room
    temperature
¾ cup white sugar
¾ cup brown sugar, firmly
    packed
2 eggs
2¼ cups all-purpose flour
½ teaspoon salt
1 teaspoon baking soda
1½ cups peanut butter
1 teaspoon vanilla extract
1 cup unsalted peanuts, chopped

1. Preheat the oven to 375°F. Lightly butter a large baking
sheet.

2. In a large bowl, with an electric mixer at high speed, beat
together the butter and both sugars until the mixture is light
and fluffy.

3. One at a time, add the eggs, mixing well after each
addition.

4. Sift together the flour, salt and baking soda. Gradually add
to the butter mixture, mixing well after each addition.

5. Mix in the peanut butter, vanilla and peanuts. Drop the
cookies by teaspoonfuls onto the prepared baking sheet, about
2 inches apart. Bake for 10 to 12 minutes.

Makes about 75 cookies

NOTES

NOTES

NOTES

NOTES

NOTES

NOTES

NOTES